Smart Parents Successful Kids

How to Get What Your Child Needs (and Deserves) from Your Local School

Suzanne Capek Tingley

Illustrated by Catherine ⁓

D1465672

Houseman Press 2015

ISBN-13: 978-0692329177

ISBN-10:069232917X

TO LARRY THE DAD

ACKNOWLEDGMENTS

REBECCA TINGLEY, LAYOUT AND DESIGN

CONTENTS

ALSO BY SUZANNE CAPEK TINGLEY

How to Deal with Difficult Parents, 2nd Ed

Chapter 1

Please See Me After Class

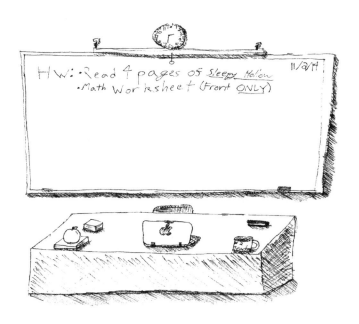

When my daughter was in seventh grade she received a failing grade on a science test. The teacher wrote on the bottom of the test, "Please have your parent sign this and make an appointment to see me."

My daughter was a good student and this was an aberration. "What happened?" I asked her.

"I don't *know*," she said through tears, mortified by the grade and even more mortified that I had to meet with her teacher.

Given my daughter's track record I thought the teacher's request was perhaps an overreaction. Still I was a conscientious parent so I took time off from work and dutifully made an appointment to meet with her teacher.

I waited in the school conference room for about ten minutes. Finally the teacher appeared, coffee mug in hand. Here's how the conversation went:

> **Teacher:** You didn't really have to come in. Your daughter is a great student.
>
> **Me:** You wrote on her test to make an appointment!
>
> **Teacher:** I wrote that on all the kids' papers. I didn't really mean Jennifer.
>
> **Me:** You are a first class jerk.

OK – I didn't say that last thing. I thought it though and hoped it didn't appear in a bubble above my head.

Here's how it really went:

> **Me:** My daughter was very upset by your note and I took off work to see you.
>
> **Teacher:** I'm sure it won't happen again.
>
> **Me:** You better believe it, buddy.

Well, OK, I didn't say that either. But I did say this:

> **Me:** By the way, how many students failed that test?
>
> **Teacher:** Nearly all of them.

Me: (Silence)

Teacher: They just didn't study.

Me: (Silence)

Teacher: I'm going to retest at the end of this week.

Me: I'm assuming you retaught the material then – maybe in a different way.

Teacher: Yes.

Me: Well, I'm sure they will do better.

Teacher: Let's hope so.

Ah, the power of silence. Or as we say in the education business, *wait time.*

A few years ago I wrote a humorous book for teachers called, *How to Deal with Difficult Parents.* In it, I talk about strategies that teachers can use to work more effectively with parents for the good of their students. Those strategies include, among other things, responding to parents' concerns, contacting parents in a timely fashion, setting realistic expectations, being specific about students' needs, and demonstrating courtesy.

I also caution teachers about ways in which their behaviors can exacerbate a problem or even cause the problem in the first place. Like calling a parent in for a conference to witness your own failure.

This book deals with the other side of the coin – the assertive behaviors parents can take to ensure that their child gets what he or she needs at school without making matters worse. I could have, for example, told my daughter's teacher that he was an uncaring idiot. I could have gone over his head to complain to the principal. I could have talked to all the other parents about him. Frankly, however, his actions, while annoying and thoughtless, didn't actually warrant any of those responses.

I admit, complaining to the principal would have given me momentary satisfaction. Yet it wouldn't have helped my child in his class. In fact, it might have caused her further problems.

In the end my daughter got what she needed – reteaching and retesting. And I got what I needed – the opportunity to nicely point out that the teacher had inconvenienced me for something that was his fault. It didn't happen again.

As parents we need to advocate for our children to ensure they are safe at school and getting the kind of education all kids deserve. Sometimes it's easy. Calling the school for an appointment is no problem. You feel welcomed when you come in. Your child's teacher listens to what you have to say. The principal clearly likes working with kids and is responsive to parents. You feel confident that school personnel are on top of any problems that might arise and are eager to work with parents to improve each child's experience. All in all, there seems to be a partnership between home and school.

Sometimes it's not so easy.

The school and the whole system seem like a labyrinth. It's hard to get an appointment with your child's teacher or the principal. The school's philosophy seems to be to stonewall every parent's request. Discipline is uneven or nonexistent. No one seems to be responsive or responsible. The principal acts like every kid is a problem. Getting what your child needs is a hassle. Sometimes you don't even know where to begin when a problem arises. It's clear that the school sees parents as adversaries.

I once worked in an unresponsive school like that. I was the new principal of the poorest school in a very poor school district. In that school young mothers often brought their own mothers with them for support when they had to meet with their child's teacher or the principal. Many of these moms and grandmothers remembered school as intimidating, even frightening. They were already angry and resentful when they came into the building. They remembered past slights, and they were determined that their child wasn't going to have the same unpleasant experiences they had.

I tried very hard to change the culture of that school to one that was more inviting to parents. I talked with teachers individually and in groups. We discussed our goals as a school. We practiced how we would conduct parent-teacher conferences.

After the first few months I was surprised and delighted to discover that most teachers were in fact eager for new, positive leadership so they could be the kind of teachers they hoped to be when they graduated from college. Parents began to attend open houses, reading nights, and school presentations. A new PTA was formed, and mothers and grandmothers began to participate in class parties and field days.

The superintendent and the central office encouraged and supported our efforts to engage parents, and before long parents felt that they were welcomed into the building as participants in their child's education. The change in the school culture was even reflected in improvement in our state test scores.

It was a win-win for everyone. School personnel can and should be partners with their students' parents. All it takes is commitment and effort on both parts.

Even if your child's school situation is not ideal, you can still find ways to get what your child needs and deserves without becoming the parent that teachers talk about in the faculty room (yes, this actually happens). You don't want your child to be the one no teacher wants as a student not because of her, but because of you. You don't want a faculty-assigned nickname such as "Always Mad Dad" (which is one of the milder ones I overheard).

As parents we need to act judiciously for maximum effectiveness – but act nonetheless. Perhaps we can even help change the culture of a school. At the very least, we can get from the school what our child needs and deserves.

Both teachers and parents sometimes forget that when the home and school work together, the child benefits. Most teachers care about kids and want to do their best for them. However, a school system can be a repository for traditional, embedded rules and behaviors that benefit the adults in the system rather than the students. Schools that have allowed their mission to drift from kids' progress to adults' comfort can pose formidable obstacles to parents who simply want to be involved in their child's education to ensure their child's success.

In this book I will share with you ideas that will work with teachers and administrators to get the best for your child. We'll talk about what to say, when to say it, and how to say it; and we'll discuss how to move up the administrative ladder as necessary. We'll also discuss how important it is for students and teachers to have positive, caring relationships whenever possible. These ideas and suggestions in this book are gleaned from my many years in education as a teacher, principal and superintendent – and most importantly, as a parent myself.

Suzanne Capek Tingley

Chapter 2

The First Bell Rings

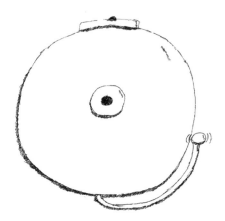

It's the first day of school.

You're standing with your child at the bus stop wondering where the time went. He's wearing new sneakers and carrying a little backpack. His face is filled with excitement mixed with a little apprehension. You are watching him with pride and your eyes are a little misty. He jumps up and down when he sees the bus coming, almost forgets to say good-bye to you in his excitement, and waves happily, if tentatively, to you from the bus window. It's a morning full of hope for both of you.

Fast Forward

Your little boy is now in third grade. He often dawdles in the morning and has missed the bus a couple of times. His teacher says he's behind in reading yet doesn't offer any extra help. She thinks he should be tested for learning problems; you think she doesn't want to take the time to give him a little extra attention.

The last parent conference didn't go well. His teacher says your son may have ADHD and should be on medication. You think he's just a normal boy. Last week he ended up in the hall for fooling around. You called the principal and asked her how your boy is supposed to learn if he's out in the hall.

Parent-Teacher conferences are coming up again and you're dreading them. What if she wants to retain him? You won't stand for it. He's only a third grader, you think. But what is fourth grade going to look like for him? Sixth grade? High school?

What happened to the little boy who couldn't wait to start school? What happened to his optimistic parents?

We all want that first day excitement about school to last forever. We want teachers who challenge our kids, who know our kids, and most of all, who like our kids. We want a school that is safe, and we want the adults at school to be fair. We want kids and teachers to sing "Don't Worry, Be Happy" as they're skipping into the building surrounded by bluebirds and friendly forest animals. At the secondary level we want them to sing, "We Are the Champions." The bluebirds and forest animals aren't really necessary at this point.

That's what we want. What we may get, if we're not mindful, are kids who need to be dragged out of bed in the morning to get on the bus. Kids who hate math or science or English and think school is boring. Kids who need help and aren't getting it. Kids who have disciplinary issues. Kids who can't wait to get out of there.

Suzanne Capek Tingley

And we get parents who are frustrated, resentful, and maybe angry. Everybody's singing the blues.

Parenting methods and teaching methods have changed over the years. Families have changed, curriculum has changed, technology has become integral to our lives, and testing has taken on a life of its own. What remains constant is the central interaction between kids and their teachers, between kids and their parents or significant adults in their lives, and between home and school. Those are the relationships that we need to focus on.

For the most part, kids don't change their attitudes about school overnight. Instead it's a slow process that may include any or all of the following: Lack of individual attention, material that is too challenging or not challenging enough, no individualized instruction, undiagnosed learning problems, disruptive behaviors from other students, poor attendance (student and teacher), teacher indifference, lack of school mission, no extra help. Generally, kids believe that their teachers are resigned to the fact that some students will inexorably fall behind. They sometimes think that nobody cares.

There are other reasons that kids don't succeed, of course, but in my experience the majority of problems center on the essential relationships between teachers and students. When those relationships are shoddy, negative, or even non-existent, students have a hard time committing to staying in school.

Because few of these issues are of the suddenly explosive variety, it's easy for a parent to miss their child's gradual apathy about school, sense of failure, or lack of expectations that anything new or exciting will occur.

Insider tip: Strong primary school instruction is key to developing positive attitudes toward school. Why? Because not only do kids learn the way the system operates, but also they learn the main skill that will determine their future success in school and maybe in life. That main skill is reading. So those first three years are crucial to your child's future success.

You can help your child get the strongest teachers in those primary grades if you understand how the system works. In many schools teachers at each grade level meet at the end of the year to distribute kids "equitably" in classes at the next level. They look at the ratio of boys to girls, and they try to put together classes with equal distributions of average ability kids, special needs kids, and gifted kids. Sometimes groups of kids with special needs or gifted kids are grouped together to make it easier for extra help or enrichment. Often twins will be put in different classes, as are siblings, if one has been retained and is now in the same grade as his brother (yet another reason to retire the archaic practice of retention).

Some schools ask parents if they have a teacher preference for their child with the caveat that the school may not be able to honor all requests. If you are new to the school, you may not know the reputations of various teachers. Staff members, however, know who the best teachers are and so does the principal.

In fact, when I was an elementary principal, one of the questions I most dreaded from new parents was, "If it were your child, which teacher would you want her to have?" I knew whom I would want my daughter to have at every grade level. The principal can't really answer that question in a straightforward manner, though, or some teachers would have classes of 60 while other teachers would have classes of 5.

So I ended up saying something vague like, "All of our teachers meet district standards and will do a good job with your child." This was absolutely true. Every teacher would do a good job. Some, however, would do an excellent job.

So if you are new to a district, try to find out which class teachers' kids are in. They will most likely have the best teachers.

While the primary grades are the first blocks in the foundation of your child's education, it's important to remember as your child moves through school, that there is never a time when he doesn't need you as an advocate, a supporter, and a participant in his school experience. Parents and teachers should be partners throughout the whole endeavor.

What often happens, however, is that parents are tremendously involved in the primary grades, less involved at middle school, and sometimes completely invisible at high school. Don't be that parent. Stay the course for your child's entire time in school.

Suzanne Capek Tingley

Chapter 3

Fifty Percent of Success Is Showing Up

Before we get into the sometimes-complicated relationships between home and school, let's talk about our basic responsibility as parents to make sure that our kids are in school and on time. After all, you can't win if you don't play the game.

The positive correlation between regular attendance and success in school seems like a no-brainer. Just in case you need statistical evidence, however, here's something to think about. The National Assessment of Educational Progress (NAEP), a test administered every two years to fourth and eighth graders across the nation, reveals that students who missed the most school in 2013 tended to score lower in math and reading than students who attended regularly. Indeed, chronically absent students in Washington, D.C., for example, scored fifteen points lower in math than students who missed no school in the month before the tests were administered (Brown, "Test Data Show Link Between Students' Scores, Absence Rates," *Washington Post*, May 4, 2014).

Regular daily attendance in school cannot be negotiable. Children learn quickly what their parents value and what they expect. Of course, children get sick and emergencies arise. Still, kids need to learn early on that as far as their parents are concerned, going to school is what kids do. We do not need to discuss this idea every morning.

If your child is particularly or unusually reluctant to go to school, you need to investigate what's going on and intervene or advocate for your child if necessary (more about that later). If it's basically that he'd rather stay home and watch Sponge Bob or surf the Internet, you need to be clear that that these are not options.

You should be aware that so-called "school phobia" is often more about home than about school. It isn't so much that kids are afraid to go to school. Instead, they worry about what will happen at home while they're gone. This is not the case for every child, of course, but it's something to keep in the back of your mind.

When I was teaching eighth grade, I had a student who was chronically late to my first period class. I was a teacher who started on time, and my students knew that when the bell rang they needed to be in their seats and ready to rock and roll. I knew that the first minutes of class are prime teaching time, so I didn't waste them by checking attendance, collecting book money, or talking about life in general. That stuff could come afterwards. The bell rang and class started.

Ten minutes later the door opened and Lester ambled in. All eyes swiveled from me to Lester as he made his grand entrance. Talking to him about being on time made no difference. A call to his mother made no difference.

Lester's Mom: It's not Lester's fault he's late.

Me: Whose fault is it?

Lester's Mom: It's mine. I need to have my coffee before I drive him to school.

Me: He could take the bus.

Lester's Mom: He could, but I prefer to drive him. It's our special time.

Well, I thought my first period English class was kind of a "special time" too, so I began locking my classroom door when the bell rang so that Lester had to stand in the hall until there was a break in the action. That worked until his mother complained to the principal that I was "unjustly punishing Lester."

I was told to unlock my door.

So Lester continued to roll in late, but I moved his seat to the one closest to the entrance, depriving him of his sashay down the aisle. Still, upon arrival, Lester noisily settled in, shuffling his papers and raising his hand to ask where we were. I ignored him. He was enjoying his little power play, and I was beginning to find it hard to like this kid.

Then, something serendipitous happened. I decided to begin each day by reading aloud to my students from a book we had chosen as a class. You might not think eighth grade kids would want to be read to, but you would be wrong. They loved it and it turned out to be a great way to settle in for the day's lesson. In fact, when I reached the end of the reading section, they frequently begged for just a little more.

So we were into the story when the door opened and Lester sauntered in. As he settled noisily into his seat, students looked over at him, annoyed, and voiced a few things teachers could only think.

Student A: Dude, shut up!

Student B: C'mon, you're interrupting the story!

Student C: Why don't you just stay home?

Class in General: *(Groans)* Not again.

After that day, Lester decided he could get to class on time.

Most teachers try to like all kids maybe not equally, but at least equally enough so that no one could ever tell which kids they like and which kids they can't warm up to. It takes a lot to really dislike a kid. I worked hard to treat Lester fairly as the year progressed, but I couldn't muster up the warmth, the joking, and the smiles the other kids got. I'm not really proud of my behavior here. Still you should know how teachers can react to this sort of thing even if they wished they didn't.

So make sure your kid is on time and in attendance every day. Teachers expect it. Just being there will not make teachers like your child, but not being there will definitely make teachers less than willing to help him when he is there. Of course, there are times when absence or tardiness just can't be helped. Make it the exception. And by the way – if your school has a policy to call parents when your child is absent, don't be annoyed. Every unnecessary call is worth it on the day your child decides to hang out with a buddy instead of showing up at school. Kids do things like that sometimes.

Suzanne Capek Tingley

Chapter 4

Save Your Energy for the Stuff That Matters

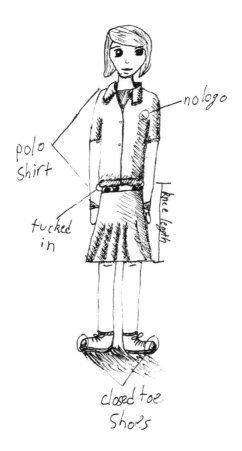

no logo

polo shirt

knee length

tucked in

closed toe shoes

What your child wears is what you and she agree on and you are willing to pay for. So if you're OK with bare midriffs and 3" platforms on a 10-year-old, so be it.

But not at school.

Some schools require uniforms, of course, and nearly all schools have a dress code. Check it out and insist that your child dress according to whatever the school expects (as long as it's not just totally arbitrary and I'll talk about that in a minute).

In my years as a school administrator, I've had many clashes with parents – usually mothers – about their child's dress despite the fact that we had a clear dress code and I tended to be more liberal about dress than some. Some fashion statements, I believe, should simply be ignored by school people. Pink hair, flip-flops in winter, tattoos, black nail polish, unusual haircuts or no hair at all – my tendency was to ignore the things that come and go. Not every administrator feels that way, of course, so be prepared if your principal has a problem with a barbed wire tattoo around your son's neck (even though there's not much you can do about that).

There are safety issues and decency standards that kids pretty much need to observe. I realize that these standards are always somewhat subjective, so let's just say that what your kid wears to school shouldn't distract from why he's there. Offensive messages on t-shirts or too much observable skin have a tendency to do that.

So rather than spending hours arguing with school administrators or the school board or threatening a lawsuit, make sure your child dresses appropriately for class. It's training for life.

I know that some parents will say that the school shouldn't try to suppress their child's individuality, but you might want to ask yourself if what he or she wants to wear to school would be OK for a large family gathering – say Thanksgiving or a family wedding or funeral.

Suzanne Capek Tingley

Save your energy for things that matter. Another question I have to raise is whether you are standing up for your child's individual rights or whether you simply don't want to confront your child yourself. Just askin'.

On the other hand, schools can cause their own problems when there is no clear dress code or when administrative decisions appear arbitrary. Every so often some administrator will make a decision like that and the next thing he knows he's on the national news looking like an idiot (for banning the "I Heart Boobies" bracelets for breast cancer awareness, for example, or enforcing a "zero tolerance" policy by suspending a second grader for wearing a baseball cap adorned with tiny plastic soldiers with tiny plastic guns).

When the decision seems to rest with the personal feelings of the principal, you may have to go in and chat with him or her about that. What your child wears to school should be based on institutional standards, not on your principal's personal beliefs. In addition, the standards need to be applied equally to all; that is, students should not be singled out by gender or gender preference, age, physical appearance, or pecking order in the school's social hierarchy.

This past fall, for example, administrators at a Richmond, Virginia high school informed students that there would soon be a shorts-length spot check. Shorts were to be fingertip length. Any girls found in violation would be forced to change. In addition, if more than 10 girls were found in violation of the dress code, all girls – not just the ones in violation – would be banned from wearing shorts for a day. (Some administrators never seem to learn that group punishment rarely has the effect they think it will.)

Although kids were understandably upset, they handled it beautifully by themselves. A couple of days later the boys arrived at school wearing tiny short shorts. Girls were modestly covered. Needless to say, not everyone was amused, but it was a non-violent, funny, and thought-provoking rebuke to sexism and inequality (Ballou, *Bustle*, October 2014).

So if you feel that the dress code is whatever the principal thinks looks good that particular day or that your child is being singled out, it's OK to sit down with him for a civil chat. The key word here is "civil."

If you are unhappy with the principal's response, you are free to move up to the administrative chain of command, even up to the board of education. State your case, but don't threaten:

> **Parent:** So I'm wondering – if there's not a school dress code, how do kids know what's acceptable and what's not?
>
> **Principal:** I make that decision.
>
> **Parent:** Isn't that kind of arbitrary?
>
> **Principal:** I've been doing this a long time and I know what kids should wear.
>
> **Parent:** Well, I guess I have to say that I just can't agree with your point of view that thin girls can wear halter-tops but chubby girls can't. I will make an appointment to talk with the superintendent and see if we can come up with a better guideline.

Believe me when I tell you that a calm, purposeful statement like this is much stronger than the following:

Suzanne Capek Tingley

Parent: This is blatant discrimination! You'll hear from my lawyer!

It is, of course, blatant discrimination and you may actually get to the point of having to hire a lawyer. But don't start out that way.

In the meantime, remember that your child can wear anything he or she wants (if you approve) outside of school. Kids are in school roughly six to seven hours a day for 180 days each year. About 85% of their lives go on outside of school in any given year. Following the dress code for the other 15% isn't all that hard.

Don't make it an issue in your child's education – unless you have to. Then go for it. Because sometimes it isn't about fashion; it's about discrimination.

Suzanne Capek Tingley

Chapter 5

Guiding and Doing Aren't the Same Thing

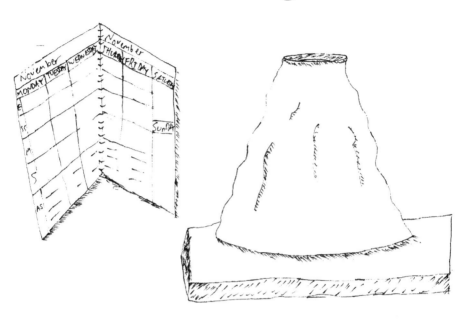

Homework

A *USA Today* survey reveals that the amount of homework that kids are assigned hasn't changed in the last 30 years (Toppo, USA Today March 18, 2014). What has changed, of course, is the number of distractions kids have and the technology they have to accomplish their homework (or to distract them).

Please note that I am not a big fan of homework for the sake of homework. Assigning all students page 54 (the odd problems) may be unnecessary for the kids who have already mastered the concept. Nor do I believe that homework should be a part of a kid's grade in the class. The grade should reflect progress towards mastery of the subject as revealed by tests, written work, or projects.

If your school gives grades for behavior (often called "citizenship" or "effort"), your child's diligence regarding homework should be part of that grade, not part of her academic grade. Remember, the academic grade should reflect how well your child has mastered the subject or progressed towards an academic goal whether she does it through homework, meditation, osmosis or watching Youtube videos. This is an argument to keep in mind when you question your child's teacher's habit of making homework 30% of your child's grade.

But I am not the Queen of Homework and I don't get to make the rules.

The reality is that many teachers still assign the same homework to everyone and include it as part of a student's grade. Now, you may want to have a conversation with your child's teacher about her homework policies (See Chapter Six, "Talking to Your Child's Teacher"). Until you speak with the teacher, however, here is a conversation you don't want to have:

> **Kid:** I hate homework. It's so boring. I already know how to spell these words so why do I have to write them five times?
>
> **Parent:** You're right. It's totally stupid.
>
> **Kid:** I'm not going to do it.
>
> **Parent:** I don't blame you. I wouldn't either.

Here's another conversation you don't want to have with your child:

> **Kid:** I hate Mr. Arletti. He assigns tons of homework and it's so boring.
>
> **Parent:** Arletti has assigned the same stuff for years.
>
> **Kid:** It's a waste of time
>
> **Parent:** Well, just do half.

When it comes to talking to your child about school, be smart. You are not your child's BFF. You are an adult, not one of your child's classmates. Even if you agree with your child's take on his homework, stick with his teacher's expectations until you talk to him or her.

Here are the main reasons for supporting the teacher regarding homework at this point:

- Homework may be part of your child's grade.

- Your child may actually need the practice.

- Your conversation with your child's teacher about homework assignments will have a greater chance of success if you're proactive rather than reactive. In other words, talk to your child's teacher before your child stops doing homework and the teacher calls you first. That way you can avoid looking either defensive or ineffective.

So your conversation with your child before you talk to his teacher should sound more like this:

Kid: Why do I have to write these words 5 times when I already know how to spell them?

Parent: I'm meeting next week with your teacher to talk about your homework assignments.

Kid: Really? Cool!

Parent: In the meantime, do the homework.

Of course, there's always the possibility that your child says this:

Kid: Uhhh, forget it. The assignment isn't so bad. I really don't mind it.

Or he might say this:

Kid: What??? Dad, no! Don't do it. I'll just write the words. I don't want Mr. Arletti to think I'm a baby.

If that happens, you have two possible responses:

Parent: Then quit complaining and do your work.

Parent: Too late. I'm seeing your teacher next week.

Of course, there is also Option Three, which is to take stock of the situation and avoid a knee-jerk reaction. If your child actually needs the practice that homework provides, help him learn that sometimes work like this is necessary to master a concept or task. If most of his assignments are helpful and not just rote learning, teach him to just finish them up and move on.

By the way, keep in mind that rote learning has gotten a bad rap during the last few years. Simple repetition and practice has

Suzanne Capek Tingley

given you some skills that have come in handy over your lifetime. Thanks to rote learning, for example, you know that 6 x 7 is 42 without having to write down a column of 7's and add them up. If you're one of the lucky people who took keyboarding, you can type swiftly instead of using two fingers. Even as an adult you go to the driving range in an attempt to groove your swing.

Many of us are familiar with Malcolm Gladwell's "10,000 Hours Rule," in which he insists that nearly anyone can become expert at a task or skill after 10,000 hours of practice. Others point out that practicing the same mistakes without correcting them makes practice useless and doesn't account for natural ability. Ten thousand hours of practice will not make me a runway model. Still, natural ability alone will not make one an expert. But I digress.

One way to help kids through an assignment is to ask your child how long she thinks the task should take. Let's say she says 15 minutes. Set a timer for 15 minutes and when the bell rings, she's done – even if she has two more problems. Chances are she'll want to go ahead and finish those last two now that she's done all the rest. Or not. Setting a timer can also help the child who dawdles or the child who is a perfectionist to move along.

But if unnecessary homework assignments are a chronic problem – if your child is pretty bright and could do more challenging work – then make an appointment to talk to his teacher. As I noted earlier, you are in a much stronger position to advocate for your child if your child has been conscientious about his work and has a strong record of accomplishment. (Believe me, teachers have met plenty of parents who think their child is "too bright" to do the work assigned even though there is no real evidence that this is true.)

But what if you talk to your child's teacher and the conversation goes something like this:

> **Parent:** I wonder if you could assign Jack a little more challenging work instead of practicing things he already knows.
>
> **Teacher:** Look, I have 25 kids in this class. I can't individualize for all of them.

Here's one way to respond to that position:

> **Parent:** I recognize you have more kids than Jack. But aren't there other kids like him who would also like a little more challenging work rather than practicing stuff they already know?
>
> **Teacher:** Well, maybe. What if some kids only had to do, say, the odd or the even problems?
>
> **Parent:** I think that would really help. I appreciate your working with us on this.

But what if the teacher says this:

> **Teacher:** The extra practice won't kill them. Jack just needs to buckle down and do it. If I let him get away with not doing his work, what about all the other kids?
>
> **Parent:** It won't kill you either to individualize a little.
>
> **Teacher:** (Silence).

Clearly it would be better not to add that last comment, but it may be time to move up the organizational ladder and have a little chat with the principal.

By the way, one of my least favorite teacher excuses is that last one: "If I let him get away with (whatever), what about all the other kids?

First of all, what exactly is he "getting away with"? Not practicing things he already knows? And what *about* all the other kids? If they know it too, great. If they don't know it, it would behoove them to practice.

It's all about individualizing instruction, which – I agree – Can cause more work for teachers. Still, the goal of homogeneous classes shouldn't be to homogenize everyone's accomplishments so that the slower kids learn more and the brighter kids learn less (many schools embrace this practice of teaching to the middle even though research shows it doesn't work). My advice to parents? Don't accept excuses. If your child needs extra help or your child needs to be challenged, work with the teacher or principal to be sure your child gets what she needs.

Projects

The fourth grade science fair always brings a smile to my face and not because it reflects the kids' ideas or work. Displays are neatly labeled, pictures are retina quality, and the research is precise. Higher-level thinking skills were required for these projects, skills that have not always been apparent in some of these kids' progress until now. The quality of students' work is unbelievable and I mean that literally—you can't really believe a kid actually did it.

Helping your child with her project is not the same as doing it. It is very hard to let your child present a project with crooked pictures, dabs of glue, and a simple hypothesis when you know that other kids will look like they're eligible for Genius Grants, but you have to refuse to be part of this kabuki dance or it will never end. And believe me, teachers aren't fooled when the kid who couldn't label the parts of a flower presents a stop motion Lego film about photosynthesis.

I once observed a second grade class in which kids had to show their classmates how to complete a simple project step by step. The students were divided into small groups and some of their mothers were there to help out. Projects ranged from how to make a peanut butter sandwich to how to make a bird feeder to how to braid a Barbie doll's hair.

In the group I observed, the girl who showed how to make a peanut butter sandwich was on her own. She had brought a loaf of white bread, a few plastic knives, and a jar of peanut butter. She doled out the bread, opened the jar, and proceeded to explain how to make the sandwich. Directions were clear, concise, and simple.

The kid who showed how to make a bird feeder was also a solo act. The project required Popsicle sticks, peanut butter (again), and birdseed. It was messy, but it was also clear, concise, and simple.

Then it was time to learn how to braid Barbie's hair.

This little girl's mom was there. The first thing Mom did was hand all 6 kids in the group a brand new Barbie doll, still in the package. Each kid also got a Barbie brush and hairband. The two boys in the group looked nonplussed, but gamely carried on.

Mom helped everybody release the Barbies from their plastic clams. Mom showed them how to CAREFULLY brush Barbie's hair. Mom demonstrated on her own child how to divide

Suzanne Capek Tingley

the hair into three strands and then how to plait it. Mom helped the kids tie the hairbands to the ends of the braids. Her little girl was silent, working on her own doll.

Mom got an A. Her daughter lost an opportunity to teach something to other kids and learn something herself in the process.

The whole experience reminded me of a time I volunteered to help in a fourth grade class for the Valentine's Day party. The kids had to cycle through "stations," a different activity at each station.

I worked with a mother who wanted kids to make interlocking hanging hearts out of various-sized wallpaper strips and brass buttons. The result was lovely, but it required concentration and dexterity some 9-years-olds couldn't quite muster up.

The boy sitting next to me watched the mom explain the task and then turned to me and asked quietly, "Do we all have to make these?" I looked around for an out for him, but before I could respond, the mom said firmly, "Yes. It will be fun."

"I'm doomed," he said.

Planning and Organization

Many schools require kids to have some kind of planner from the time they are in upper elementary school. Planners can be paper or digital, and I would encourage you as a parent to help your child get into the habit early (say, third or fourth grade) of keeping some kind of simple planner. In the early grades it could be a couple of pages in a folder for homework assignments, tests and projects. Later many schools may require kids to have a planner or even a computer program for daily use.

Many elementary teachers send home a type of "Friday letter" to inform parents about classroom events or to share specific information about their child. Check your child's folder.

As kids get older, they will take on more responsibility for keeping their own planners. It's not a bad idea to check on those now and then since often parents don't get much information about their child's progress until the child is failing.

The most important thing is to talk to your child about school and I don't mean like this:

> **Parent:** How was your day?
>
> **Student:** Fine.
>
> **Parent:** Great. We're having pork chops for dinner.

Or this:

> **Parent:** What did you learn in school today?
>
> **Student:** Nothing.
>
> **Parent:** Huh. Well, we're having pork chops for dinner.

Conversations about school should be ongoing. Remember that general questions like "How are things going?" will often elicit a one-word response like this: "Fine." On the other hand, if you know a little more about your child's life at school, you can say, "What do you think will be on your science test?" Questions like that require more than one word (although it could be, "Beats me").

Here's another example of how to encourage your child to talk about the day's events:

Parent: Did you give your book report today?

Student: No, it's tomorrow.

Parent: Did anyone give one today?

Student: Yeah, Miley and Lee.

Parent: How did that go?

Student: I don't think Miley actually read her book.

Yes, it turns out that oral book reports are still around, despite the fact that they are always in the top ten most boring activities for everyone involved including the teacher.

I remember a book report I did in high school. Not only had I not read the book, the book didn't exist. I made up the title, the author, and the plot. Because I was a good, dependable student, I got away with it. After my oral report the teacher said, "It sounds like a very exciting story."

Yes, it certainly was.

This was the first, but not the only time I used this ploy. I also made up a written report about Vasco de Gama that included his playing in a rock band in his early years. My lab report after the frog dissection included how sad it was that no princess would ever kiss him.

These were invaluable, if dishonest, academic lessons for me as a student and as the teacher I would later become. I learned not to assign work I didn't plan to read. Again, I digress.

Here's another way to talk to your child about school:

> **Parent:** How much reading do you have to do for tomorrow?
>
> **Student:** I don't know. Some.
>
> **Parent:** Are you going to do it before or after dinner?
>
> **Student:** I guess after.
>
> **Parent:** OK. By the way, we're having pork chops.

By now you're asking, what's with the pork chops? Just a little joke, but there is a hidden message. It suggests that you'll be having dinner together with your child, an activity I heartily recommend. Also, I heartily recommend no smartphones or earbuds at the table. Otherwise, it doesn't matter what you're having because everyone is eating alone.

Tests

The reason that I talked about planning before talking about tests is that you can help your child prepare for tests if you know when they are. With some kids all a parent has to say is, "Remember you have your science test on Friday." Other kids will need a little more assistance depending on their organizational skills. You may need to say, "Remember you have your science test on Friday, which is the day after tomorrow." Posting on your own calendar may be useful.

Keep in mind, though, that it's your child's test, not yours. That is easier said than done if the conversation goes something like this:

Suzanne Capek Tingley

Parent: Seth, don't you have a math test tomorrow?

Seth: Uh, I don't know. Maybe.

Parent: Get your planner (or phone) and let's look.

Seth: Yeah, it looks like it's tomorrow.

Parent: What's it on?

Seth: Not sure. Fractions maybe?

If you go over your child's planner with him at the beginning of the week, it's more likely that the conversation may go a little more like this:

Parent: Seth, don't you have a math test tomorrow?

Seth: Yeah, I think so.

Parent: Are you ready for it?

Seth: Yeah, I think so.

Parent: Where's your book?

Seth: I think it's in my locker.

I didn't say the plan was foolproof.

Still, many kids need help with planning and deadlines, particularly in middle school when they have more classes, more changes, and, of course, puberty to deal with. As kids move towards high school they become more independent and more responsible for their own learning (at least that's the goal). Middle schoolers, however, aren't there yet.

Back to tests. You can help your child be aware of when they occur and you can help your child prepare for them if she is OK with your help. Sometimes just the reminder is impetus to review. In any event, keep abreast of your child's progress by asking how she did on the test and whether she was happy with her score.

Throughout my years in education, I met many parents who claimed to be completely unaware that their son or daughter was failing a particular subject. Even when teachers sent out several notices, some parents still insisted they had no idea.

I've also known parents who were astounded to discover a few days before graduation that their child would not be walking across the stage because she had failed to complete work for a required course. Relatives are already on their way, party invitations have been sent, and their child has been accepted to college...but graduation for that student will not happen until summer school is completed in August.

Don't be that parent.

Check the planner, ask your child how she's doing, attend parent conferences, and don't believe all your child tells you. Involvement in your child's daily life at school is so important (and this is such a long chapter) that I'm going to give you a quick review before we leave the topic:

- The basics are not negotiable.

- Your child needs to be in school and on time unless there are extenuating circumstances. He or she needs to be dressed appropriately.

- Support your child's work, but don't do it for him.

Suzanne Capek Tingley

•Keep track of your child's progress. Know when important projects or tests are due.

•Let your child take responsibility for her learning. Your role is to guide and support.

Now let's talk about how and when to talk to your child's teacher.

Suzanne Capek Tingley

Chapter 6

Talking to Your Child's Teacher

Communicating with your child's teacher can be a minefield. If you make a wrong move, a simple problem can explode into an unpleasant and ongoing issue that may make matters worse instead of better.

The first rule for parents when dealing with a problem at school is this: Remain civil. The second rule is to start at the lowest level and follow the chain of command. The third rule is to remain civil. So is the fourth rule, and probably the fifth as well.

Just to reiterate, if your child is having difficulties at school – academic or social – start with your child's teacher, NOT THE PRINCIPAL. You will note that I rarely shout, but nothing aggravates a teacher more than when a parent goes to the principal first without even giving her a chance to deal with the problem.

When I was a principal I routinely told parents who called me first that they had to talk to the teacher before I would deal with their complaint. My policy did not make some of them happy, but parents who had real concerns did contact the teacher. Others felt they had made their complaint known and that was enough.

Not every principal embraces that point of view, however, and some will listen to a parent's complaint about a teacher and then talk to the teacher in an attempt to resolve the issue. This move saves parents from having to confront the teacher, but let me say again, it will not endear you to the teacher and it may result in negative consequences for your child. So instead of calling the principal, contact the teacher first.

Please note that I am talking here about problems that the teacher has the ability to solve or at least work on – issues like your child's academic progress, bullying, homework, the need for testing or extra help, etc. However – and this is a big HOWEVER – if you suspect that your child's teacher has behaved in an inappropriate or unprofessional manner that might endanger your child or anyone else's, go directly to the principal and move on up the ladder as necessary. Do it as soon as you suspect something might be happening even if it's at night or on a weekend – and even if you think untoward behavior could never happen in your school.

Suzanne Capek Tingley

The Right Time

If your child is having a problem in the classroom – academic, social, or behavioral – you'll want to have a serious, private, and professional conversation with your child's teacher. It is not possible to have a conversation that meets these criteria – namely, serious, private, and professional – in these situations:

- at the grocery store

- at the liquor store

- at a party

- during open house at school

- in the school parking lot

- at a basketball game

- in the lingerie section of your local Macy's

- after church

- at Target, particularly while waiting in the pharmacy

- in the doctor's office

- on vacation at the Outer Banks or anywhere else.

- at the hair salon.

You get the picture.

Once when I was looking for blinds at Home Depot on a Saturday afternoon I spotted one of my students and her parent in the next aisle. I tried to hide behind the floor lamps, but unfortunately the woman spotted me and came right over, dragging the child behind her.

> **Parent:** Hi, Ms. Tingley. I'm so glad we ran into you. Sarah doesn't really understand why she had lunch detention yesterday and I hope you can explain it to her.

> **Me:** Well, Sarah, as I told you very plainly at school, you raked your nails down a classmate's neck when she wouldn't give you her chips at lunch. Does that ring a bell?

Just wanted to see if you were paying attention. I didn't say that. Not because it wasn't true, but because it was Saturday and I was on my own time and I couldn't decide whether getting real wood blinds instead of plastic faux wood was worth the price. Here's what I really said:

> **Me:** It's nice to see you. But right now I'm shopping for blinds. Please call me on Monday and I'll be happy to chat with you.

Sarah's mother wasn't happy. She gave me the fish eye and an icy, "Oh, all right then, I will." Happily, she never did. I ended up with the faux wood blinds and they looked just fine.

The lesson here is that if you accost a teacher on her own time, she is likely to think it's a "gotcha" moment and will feel resentful that you are disrespectful of her privacy. So call the school and set up an appointment or email or text your child's teacher if that is an accepted protocol. It really works out better.

Comments to Avoid

When you do talk to your child's teacher, you might want to keep in mind this short list of things that you probably don't want to say unless you really want to annoy the teacher and consequently make matters worse. The list includes:

- "He never does that at home."

- "He needs to be challenged. He acts out because he's bored."

- "We're going on vacation a few days before school break. Can you get some work together for my son?"

- "Your tests are too hard."

- "You give too much homework."

- "It's hard to really understand kids if you don't have any of your own."

- "Just remember: I pay your salary."

- "My daughter needs you to write a reference for her college application. Can you have it by Friday?"

Here's my all-time favorite: "My daughter says that you yell at her for things other kids get away with. *I'd like to hear your side of the story.*" Like the child and I are equals on the playground and the parent is going to mediate.

Teachers could probably come up with lots of other comments that set their teeth on edge, but I'm sure you understand. What's important for parents to remember is that insulting or demeaning your child's teacher will not get your child what he or she needs to succeed any more than insulting your doctor or your hair dresser or your auto mechanic will ensure excellent service. Instead, think about how you can best work together as teammates, not adversaries.

By the way, it's not as if teacher' comments never make parents shake their heads or in the worst case, make them want to leap over the desk and shake the teacher. As a parent, I've heard some of these very comments myself, and I worked hard to keep my feet on the floor and my hands on the arms of the chair. Let me give you a few examples:

- "He doesn't seem to like math." *Huh. He loved it last year.*

- "I've had to remove her from the classroom." *How come no one called me?*

- "He doesn't seem interested in reading." *He reads at home all the time. He reads in the car. He reads in bed. He would read at the dinner table if I'd let him.*

- "She seems more interested in her social life than in chemistry." *No kidding. What kid isn't?*

- "She's very shy." *Is this a criticism or an observation?*

- "She does very well on tests but she doesn't do all her assignments." *And so the problem is...?*

- "He can be easily distracted." *Have you read his IEP? He's ADHD!*

- "I have to say he reminds me a lot of his brother." *He doesn't have a brother.*

Suzanne Capek Tingley

- "She often rushes through her work so she can read." *Sounds like the reading is a lot more interesting.*

- "She needs to get more serious about her studies." *She's seven. She has a whole lifetime to get serious.*

- "He really wants to take AP English next year, but I can't recommend him." *Let him take it. Maybe he wants the challenge. He can always go back to regular English. Why exclude him?*

Email, Texts, and Social Media

Many schools today encourage teachers to communicate with students and parents via email or texts. Some even have specific websites for the very purpose of home/school communication. When used correctly, these kinds of communication can be useful for all concerned.

As you are probably well aware, email and texts can convey unintended feelings or emotions if used carelessly. If you choose to communicate with your child's teacher via email or texts, you will want to keep a few guidelines in mind:

- If you are angry or annoyed, do not press "send" immediately after writing. Instead, wait a couple of hours and then reread what you've written. Ask someone else to read it too or if there's no one else around, read it out loud to yourself.

When I was a superintendent I had a pact with another superintendent who was a friend of mine. If either of us had to send a letter or email regarding a contentious issue, we would first send it to the other. More than once we advised one another to "Put that one in your desk drawer and leave it there."

•Do not use all capitals, which looks like you are shouting and may be a crazy person. Do not use exclamation points at the end of your sentences (there is a reason that proofreaders call exclamation points "screamers").

•Use spellcheck. Use real words, not "N BTW U R giving 2 much HW!!!

•Do not email every day or every time the spirit moves you. Your emails will carry more weight if you contact the teacher only for important matters.

•Yes, they're cute, but do not use emoticons. Ever. Especially the angry ones. These little faces may be OK for family and friends, but keep in mind that your child's teacher and you have a professional relationship.

•If you are indeed angry or annoyed or if your child has an ongoing problem that requires daily communication, make an appointment to talk to your child's teacher face-to-face. The written word sometimes conveys unintended meaning.

•Make an appointment with your teacher by calling the school secretary, not your child's teacher's cellphone. There are two big reasons to call the school secretary. First, it's a more professional way to set up an appointment. Second, some teachers really hate to talk to parents face-to-face and will try to just have a chat over the phone. Sometimes that works; often it doesn't.

I am a strong believer in sitting down and talking about a problem your child might have and working on solutions together with your child's teacher. If you are focusing on a chronic problem, a face-to-face meeting allows you to take notes and put in writing the plans that you have agreed upon.

It's often a good idea to meet for the first time in the classroom, which is a more informal setting and less intimidating to teachers who hate to meet with parents.

> •You will endear yourself to your child's teacher by sending a positive or appreciate note now and then. Example: "Sybil loved the field trip to the farm. Thank you." Stop there. Any more is sucking up.

Making Conferences Productive

Whether you have asked specifically to meet with your child's teacher or you are merely attending the annual teacher/parent conference, think about what you want to know or what goal you have in mind. The conference should be about sharing information and making plans to improve your child's progress. If you are like most parents, what you really want to know are these basic things:

> •How is my child progressing in relation to the other kids in his class?

> •Does my child get along with other kids? Does he have friends?

> •Does my child participate in class discussions or activities?

Sometimes teachers have a game plan for conferences and try to stick to the same script, with minor adjustments, for every parent they see. They forget that parents want to know more about their child than simply how well he performs on tests. So before you go into a conference, think about what you want to know and don't be afraid to ask questions.

> **Teacher:** John scored in the 82nd percentile in math and the 79th percentile in reading.

> **Parent:** So is that what you would expect from him? Could he do better or is he working at capacity?

Here's another example:

> **Teacher:** Alex is a hard worker and contributes a lot to class discussion.

> **Parent:** Does she get along with other kids?

Remember that parent conferences are for you, the parent, so make sure that you get the information you want and need. Keep in mind that if you don't get the information you want and need, you might want to move up the organizational ladder.

Also, beware of "Eduspeak." Sometimes teachers assume that you understand the current educational jargon and will use it freely in discussions with parents. If you don't know what the teacher is talking about, say so.

> **Teacher:** Julie scored 87 on the reading reliability test and appears to be able to use scaffolding to plan her writing responses.

> **Parent:** I don't know what that means, actually. Please explain.

Here's another example:

Suzanne Capek Tingley

Teacher: Ralph understands the basic math concepts but doesn't use the manipulatives appropriately.

Parent: And manipulatives would be...?

Teacher: Small plastic figures that indicate ones, tens, or hundreds.

Parent: How does he use them inappropriately?

Teacher: He sticks them in his ears or nose, sets them up for field goals, pretends they're aliens...

Parent: If they were aliens, they wouldn't be MANipulatives, would they?

You will probably want to keep that last comment to yourself.

Keep in mind that some teachers try not to deliver bad news to parents or they will try to sugarcoat it in a misguided attempt not to hurt anyone's feelings (or not to tick anyone off). If you feel that your child's teacher is dancing around a problem, you need to ask her directly what's going on.

Parent: When you say that Zach "could sometimes make better choices," what exactly does that mean? That he should buy a sandwich rather than a Milky Way for lunch or that he should stop punching his classmate when you tell him to?

Well, maybe watch the sarcasm, but make sure you come away with a clear understanding of the situation. One of my favorite ways to cut to the chase is this:

Teacher: Sometimes Pete seems to have difficulty staying on task.

Parent: What does that look like?

What does that look like? In other words, describe his specific behavior in plain English so I know what you're talking about.

It's important to get what you need from conferences so that you don't end up surprised that your child is failing or in need of special help in some way. The earlier you have this information, the better it will be for your child and for you.

A parent can sometimes feel cowed at conferences, especially if the teacher sits behind her desk and you have to sit in one of the kids' seats. This choice on the teacher's part is poor form and to my mind, a little defensive, but objecting may be awkward. Still, it's OK to say, "Are there any more grown-up chairs?" Smile because you've made your point.

Whatever the seating arrangements, don't be afraid to interrupt the teacher's set speech to get the information you want. The annual parent/teacher conferences are often time-limited, so you may have to ask to set up another appointment if you feel your child needs more discussion. Extra time to discuss your child's progress and possible needs is your right as a parent, so don't be afraid to ask for it.

Group Conferences

When your child moves to middle school or high school, she will have not just one or two teachers, but as many as seven or eight. Some schools (and parents) like to schedule group conferences to give the parent a thorough picture of their child and frankly, to save time.

If your child is an excellent student and you know you're only going to get a round table of praise for her and for your outstanding parenting skills, a group conference may work out just fine. But let me give you an **insider tip**. Sometimes a group of teachers who are having a difficult time with a student either academically or behaviorally will request a group conference with the parent. Teachers sometimes believe that if the parent hears how awful the child is doing from a whole group, the parent will be forced to take some action. In the worst-case scenario teachers will leave feeling satisfied that they got THAT of their collective chest and you will leave feeling devastated, angry, or resentful.

In the OTHER worst-case scenario, when several teachers have been very critical of your child, other teachers will begin to feel bad for you or your kid and will back off or sugarcoat real problems. Bottom line: If your child is struggling in any way, you are far better off to refuse the group conference and meet individually with her most important teachers.

One last point: Be sure you attend all scheduled conferences. If you have a conflict, see if you can set up another time with your child's teacher or conference by phone if you just can't make it to school. Communication is essential if you want to be actively engaged in your child's progress. Parents who show up or stay in touch earn the teachers' respect and cooperation.

Suzanne Capek Tingley

Chapter 7

When Your Child Has a Disciplinary Issue

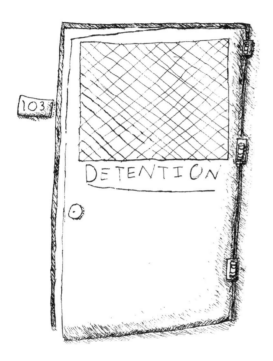

Some elementary teachers use the "pull the stick" method of discipline. Each child has a small envelop with his or her name on it tacked to the bulletin board. At the start of each day, there is a green stick in each child's envelope. The green stick symbolizes that each child is ready to go with the day's learning. If a child gets into trouble for some reason, she will be told to "pull a stick" – usually a yellow one – and replace her green one with it. The yellow, of course, means "caution." Should the child move heedlessly to the next offense, she has to replace the yellow stick with a red one and face some kind of disciplinary consequence depending on the seriousness of the offense.

This plan works reasonably well in elementary school, and for the most part parents have no involvement in it unless the dreaded red stick has to be pulled.

While the particulars may differ, the general disciplinary idea is the same in most schools K-12. Kids start fresh every day. If they misbehave in a garden-variety kind of way, they get a warning. If they continue to misbehave, the red stick morphs into removal from class, detention, suspension, or a hearing.

If you are very fortunate, your child will enter kindergarten and graduate thirteen years later with a small collection of yellow sticks and maybe one or two red sticks. If your child seems to have a penchant for red sticks, you'll need to develop more strategies to work with both your child and the school.

But let's start first with the more common infractions – disrespect, fighting, truancy, disobedience, etc. First of all, it is instinctual for most parents to want to defend their child, even if you're not so sure the child wasn't at least a little at fault. Still, if you get a call from school, it is best to remain calm and maybe even noncommittal until you get all the facts (or at least all the facts that you can get).

Here are a few comments you'll want to avoid making right off the bat:

• "What discipline is the other kid getting?"

•"What did the teacher say to my son to make him unhappy?"

•"You have no right to discipline my child."

•"I want a meeting with the other kid and his parents."

•"You people are always picking on my child."

•"Where was the teacher when this happened?"

•"I'm going to the TV station (the police, my lawyer, my congressperson, etc.)"

•"My child would never lie. If he said he didn't do it, I believe him."

You get my drift. With comments like these the battle lines are drawn and you start looking like a crazy person. You will also encourage school people to think, "No wonder his kid is like he is" (whatever that means).

Instead, when the school calls, ask questions that will clarify for you what actually occurred:

•Can you tell me exactly how this happened?

•When did this happen?

•Who else was involved?

•What exactly did my child say or do?

•What exactly will happen next?

•After I talk to my child I may want to talk with you again. When is a good time?

I know, I know. A few of you are rolling your eyes. It's a lot easier said than done. Not long ago a local school psychologist's sixth grade daughter poured her bright blue slushie over the head of another kid who kept bugging her at lunch. Both were sent to the office, and since the psychologist was working at the school that day, the principal called her and asked her to come to the office. Her daughter got two days of lunch detention.

"It was all I could do not to say, 'And how many days is the other kids getting?'" the psychologist said. "Because actually, I'm kind of proud of her for standing up for herself. But I know you can't just let kids pour slushies on other kids' heads without consequences."

As it turned out, "Slushie Girl" enjoyed a bump in her coolness factor as far as members of her class were concerned, which sort of made the whole thing worth it. She went on to a career as an illustrator and did not end up in reform school.

But I am well aware that it takes enormous self-control to ask reasonable questions in a reasonable tone of voice. A calm, civil tone at this stage is much more powerful and effective than losing your temper and insulting people. You can always do that later.

For now, however, sit down with your child and have a low-keyed conversation that doesn't include screaming or yelling or threatening or badmouthing the school. In other words, be the strong parent who lets your child know that you support her, but that part of your job as a parent is to teach her to do the right thing.

Let's say, for example, that your son's teacher asked him repeatedly to stop punching his classmate on the arm. He had to give his friend one more hard punch and that's when his friend smacked him back. Well, you'd have to think, your child deserved what he got.

But what if your conversation with your child goes something like this:

> **Mom:** What made you think it was OK to keep punching Sam in the arm?
>
> **Child:** He kept calling me an A-hole.
>
> **Mom:** Why didn't you tell your teacher?
>
> **Child:** I tried to tell her but she told me to go to the office.

OK, maybe it's time to have a chat with your child's teacher. A low-keyed conversation, of course.

On occasion a parent may get a call from an angry or frustrated administrator that sounds like this:

> **Principal:** I am sick and tired of having to talk to your child about being disrespectful to his teachers.
>
> **Parent:** And I'm sick and tired of hearing how sick and tired you are!

Well, that's going to end well.

If the principal or other administrator calls you with all guns blazing, start with something like this:

> **Parent:** I'd like to talk with you about this, but I have to insist on a civil tone.

If that doesn't slow him down, you have the right to say something like this:

> **Parent:** I'm coming to school to pick up my child. We can talk then. I'm hanging up now.

Not every principal is above trying to berate or intimidate a parent when his or her child has demonstrated a pattern of unruly behavior or has just committed an egregious disciplinary offense. Some principals, especially at the secondary level, will take those behaviors as a personal affront, making it difficult to discuss things civilly.

For example, a parent related to me this exchange he had with a high school principal when his daughter had a disciplinary issue:

> **Principal:** I intend to do everything within my power to make sure your daughter isn't disrespectful to Mr. Wallace ever again.

> **Dad:** I don't expect you to do everything within your power. I expected you to do everything that is *appropriate*.

That's what I'm talking about.

Nothing good or productive can come from a principal and parent screaming at one another. Take your child home and set up a meeting the following day when people are calmer. In the meantime, of course, have a serious talk with your child so you don't go in without all the information and risk looking like a fool. In fact, tell your child that you are counting on her to be truthful with you so that you don't go in with a disadvantage.

Unfortunately, not all disciplinary issues are simple. Many at the secondary level particularly are serious and may have heavy consequences.

Suppose, for example, your son and his friends think it would be really funny to make up an unflattering Facebook page for one of their teachers. Suppose your daughter tells a teacher to go f--- herself. Suppose she plagiarizes her last paper. Suppose your son skips school to smoke pot. Suppose your daughter arrives drunk to a school dance. Suppose your daughter accidentally hits a teacher's car in the parking lot but doesn't tell him. Suppose your son and his girlfriend are found in the auditorium's projection booth getting to know one another better. Suppose your daughter breaks an opposing point guard's nose in a post-game fight. Suppose your son robs the soda machine. Suppose he's found with a bag of pot he plans to sell to his friends. Suppose your kid urinates in another student's bottle of ice tea and doesn't tell him and thinks it's pretty funny when the kid takes a swig of it.

I've dealt with all of these issues (no, not with just my own personal kids, thank heavens!). Here's another: Suppose your son and another boy are fighting in the hall and hit the freight elevator door, knocking it off its track and into the elevator itself, trapping two custodians inside the tiny, dark, airless box for four hours.

Kids do not always make the best choices, as someone already observed.

But here's the thing: Usually the issue is bad enough the way it is without having an angry, hostile parent or an angry, hostile principal adding to the mix. So the longer you can stay calm and civil, the better the chance for a reasonable resolution.

Your job as a parent is to make sure that your child gets an impartial hearing and that any disciplinary consequences fit the infraction. It's fair to say that school administrators sometimes overreact. I've seen it happen more than a few times. A kid comes to school with pink hair or a heavy chain and the principal decides to suspend him. A student cheats on one test and fails the entire course. A student is denied a ticket to the prom because he invited a same sex date. A student finally talks back to a teacher who has been rude and disrespectful to her for weeks and ends up in detention. A second grader chews a Danish into the shape of a gun and gets suspended for a week.

You as the parent need to make sure that the consequences of your child's behavior are reasonable and that his or her civil rights are protected. So when your kid makes a significant mistake and faces discipline, you need to help the child accept the results of a poor choice while still insisting that the consequences are fair and reasonable.

> **Principal:** As a result of her disrespectful language, your child is suspended for a day.

> **Parent:** I understand that she violated the code of conduct and she will apologize to Mr. Smith.

Still, what if you confront your child and you find out that Mr. Smith has been disrespectful to her for weeks? What if he's made sarcastic comments to the class about your child? What if he's made her the brunt of his jokes? What if he has a crappy nickname for your child?

> **Principal:** Your child will be suspended for one day.

Parent: I understand, but Mr. Smith has said some pretty awful things to Beth.

Principal: For example?

Parent: He told her she's too stupid to find her way out of a box.

Principal: What??

Parent: He also told her she must be on drugs to ask a question that dumb. And he calls her "Bonza," which he says is the feminine form of Bonzo.

Does any of this excuse your child's disrespect? Possibly. At the very least, this explains it. Clearly, there's more to the story.

Maybe it's time for you, your child, the principal, and Mr. Smith to sit down and have a little chat. Actually, it's past time because you should have talked to Mr. Smith the very first time he said something inappropriate to your daughter (assuming you knew about it).

But what if the principal says this:

Principal: I find it hard to believe Mr. Smith would ever say anything like that.

If that's the case, you need to *insist* on a meeting. Because if he didn't say it and your child isn't telling the truth, you'll want to know. But if he did say it, now we're looking at a teacher disciplinary issue.

So you, your child (or just you if your child is reluctant), the principal and Mr. Smith meet. Mr. Smith vehemently denies ever saying anything unkind to your child. Perhaps he says he was just kidding and thought that everyone, including your daughter, knew it.

First of all, don't buy the "just kidding" defense. Your child didn't think it was funny.

Secondly, see if your child can get any other students to corroborate her story (of course, you need to talk to their parents before getting them involved in this issue). Let's say that one or two students agree that Mr. Smith made inappropriate remarks to your child and are willing to support her. That would certainly make your case easier and would go a long way towards curtailing the teacher's behavior.

But what if the other kids either refuse to get involved or deny ever hearing Mr. Smith say anything negative to your child? You, however, still believe she is telling the truth.

Sometimes just "delivering the message" to the teacher is enough to change behavior. Other times you may want to move up the administrative ladder to lodge your complaint with the principal's supervisor. Be prepared for the possibility that no action will be taken against the teacher if it is just your word against his. Your other course of action is to request that your child be assigned to another teacher, assuming that your child's schedule will accommodate a switch and that a similar class is currently being offered.

The plain truth is that if your child has no corroborating evidence, she will still have to take the penalty for talking back to the teacher. However, the chance of Mr. Smith ever saying something rude to your child again has been greatly reduced or eliminated. This may be small consolation, but it may be as far as you can go without more evidence.

Insider Tip: You should also be aware that sometimes disciplinary action towards the teacher might in fact occur after an incident like this. You will not know about it, nor should you. But many administrators will confront the teacher privately either because they suspect there may be some truth in your accusation, or the teacher has a history of this kind of behavior, or they don't want any more problems like this in case it actually happened. Just because you don't know about the principal's actions, don't assume that nothing happened.

Suzanne Capek Tingley

Chapter 8

When Your Child Has

Special Needs

If you think your child may have special learning needs, don't wait until he or she is struggling in school to talk to your child's teacher. Ask the teacher to arrange for testing with the school psychologist to see if your child qualifies for special help.

Be aware that schools have thirty days to comply with your request.

Many schools today offer a range of special education services to help kids keep up with their peers. Most of those services don't depend on the child being removed from his regular classroom since federal law requires that children be educated in the least restrictive environment (Individuals with Disabilities Education Act or IDEA).

Special education meetings with school personnel and parents can sometimes be contentious or just generally unpleasant. In my experience, problems arise from both sides of the table. School personnel may be defensive regarding what they consider unrealistic expectations on the part of the parent. Parents may be frustrated by their child's lack of progress or by what they perceive as an unwillingness on the part of school personnel to provide what their child needs. Parents may also wonder if the school has set high enough expectations for their child.

It helps to remember that most special education services come under state or federal guidelines regarding what can be provided and under what conditions. So take time to know which services your child qualifies for and which services he probably doesn't.

On the other hand, don't be intimidated by school personnel who may outnumber you by a considerable margin at meetings. Keep in mind that you are supposed to be working together for the good of your child, so ask questions and insist that any educational jargon be explained in layman's terms. You will need to sign off on your child's IEP (Individual Education Plan), so make sure you understand and agree with the plan before you do so.

If your child is being tested for the first time, make an appointment with the school psychologist to go over the results of the testing before you meet with the entire group of educators to establish your child's learning plan. You should not have to hear for the first time that your child is a disabled learner in front of 6-10 people you barely know.

As a school administrator I routinely reminded teachers that they were responsible for reading and implementing a student's IEP. Nonetheless, on occasion it became abundantly (and embarrassingly) clear when we met with parents that the teacher was unfamiliar with the child's plan.

When this happens, parents have a right to be annoyed, even angry. Still, it's important to stay civil because browbeating your child's teacher will not improve her relationship with your child. It's OK to ask outright if the teacher is familiar with your child's IEP, however, because she definitely should be.

If your child qualifies for special education services, your work as a parent doesn't end there. Make sure you attend all meetings to discuss your child's progress, but also check regularly with your child to see if additional services are actually making a difference. Resource Room, for example, especially at the high school level, can occasionally resemble a small study hall or lounge instead of a learning situation if it isn't carefully monitored.

Check with your child's regular education teacher regarding your child's progress and ask whether the teacher sees a difference in your child's preparation once he begins receiving services. The regular education teacher and the special education teacher should be in communication about your child's work. Ask your regular education teacher if she talks to the special education teacher. The two of them are supposed to coordinate their efforts to improve your child's learning.

If you are seeing no progress in your child's work, don't be afraid to ask what the problem is. If you are dissatisfied with the answer, you can always request a hearing, an experience schools would prefer to avoid if possible. The important thing is to be realistic, civil, and calm. You must be an advocate for your child, and you must present a composed and assertive persona. You will be working with school personnel for several years, so getting the reputation as a crazy person will not enhance your child's chances at a first-rate education.

Keep in mind that your child, like all children, has a right to a free and appropriate education, a concept school people may refer to as FAPE. A conflict sometimes arises when a school has a limited budget and parents interpret FAPE as the best education money can buy. The key words are "free and appropriate." Still, be assertive, even aggressive as you advocate for your child because what your child ends up with sometimes depends on how strongly you advocate for her. All schools operate under financial constraints, and special education services constitute an increasingly large part of the budget. Still, you can get what your child needs and deserves if you understand how the system works and what she is entitled to.

If you are bringing an advocate with you to your child's special education meetings, choose carefully so that the person you bring helps, rather than hinders your position. You want to develop strong and positive relationships with your child's teachers and other school personnel, and you should set the tone for your advocate and not let that person speak for you. The advocate should support your position and perhaps provide information that might not be readily available to you. The best advocates can be helpful to both you and the school in forming and evaluating your child's educational plan.

Your child with special needs deserves a strong educational program. Working to develop it will take time, effort, and commitment on everyone's part.

Suzanne Capek Tingley

Chapter 9

When Your Child Is a Student Athlete

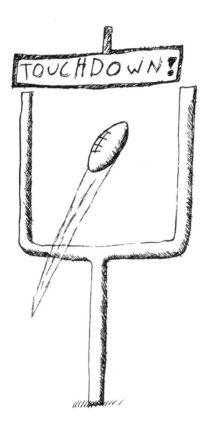

My daughter played four years of high school soccer and three years of middle school soccer. Sometimes she started, sometimes not. But she always played.

Smart Parents, Successful Kids

When she was a senior, about midway through a losing season, her coach decided to start planning for the following year. Consequently, several seniors sat the bench while freshmen or sophomores played.

My daughter handled it well. Me, not so well.

Things came to a head the day my daughter's grandparents from out of state came to see her last game. With one quarter to play, she still hadn't gotten on the field and we were losing badly. So I violated my own rules and went up to the coach on the sideline.

> **Me:** Coach, the game's not even close. My daughter's grandparents from out of state are here to see her play. Any chance you can put her in?
>
> **Coach:** (Silence)

Yes, she ignored me. That's when I picked up the nearest soccer ball and heaved it at her head (in my mind, of course). My daughter didn't play.

Years later I was on the other side of the argument when I was a superintendent. A group of parents came to the board of education to complain that the boys' basketball coach wasn't giving seniors enough playing time. I understood their concerns, but now I saw it differently:

> **Parent:** Our boys are seniors. They've earned the right to start or at least to play. We want the board to make a policy that seniors get to play.
>
> **Me:** If parents get to tell coaches which kids to play, we won't have any coaches.

So there you have it. Parents can make suggestions, but in the end varsity coaches have to make the call.

This rule is not so ironclad in elementary school, middle school, or even junior varsity. Coaches will tell you (and I agree) that the focus of the varsity team is to win games. Up to that level, however, kids are still developing the skills to play.

In my district the rule at elementary and middle levels was that all kids got to play. Everybody got a chance to start at least once during the season. In fact, years later when my daughter coached middle school soccer, she made a schedule in which every girl started at least once and everyone got the same amount of playing time. They were undefeated for the season. So it can be done.

One of the best varsity soccer coaches I ever worked with played everyone. He had an amazing ability to turn uncoordinated, even sluggish kids into athletes. And he won. So again, it can be done.

This coach's ability to take kids to the next level was extraordinary. Likewise, the varsity basketball coach in my district had a winning record every single year, not because parents in the district consistently sent him amazing athletes, but because he knew how to develop kids into athletes. Coaches like these are rare in K-12 athletics.

Unfortunately, many coaches lack the ability to develop average kids into players. They take the kids with natural ability and coach the game, not the kids. The funny thing is, it's sometimes harder for coaches to improve the skills of kids with great natural ability than it is to improve the skills of kids with average or less than average ability.

So back to your role as a parent. As I said, coaches like to win, and they don't want to be told by parents (or anyone else) how to do their job. But they can be influenced. If you feel your child isn't getting a fair break on a team, talk to the coach. Here are three major rules to keep in mind when you do:

•Before you make an appointment to talk to the coach, ask your child how he or she feels about it. Some kids would be mortified. They know their coach better than you do, and they may be afraid of looking like a baby or jeopardizing what playing time they do have. So if your child says no, honor his or her wishes.

•Don't talk to the coach before, during, or after a game.

•Don't criticize his or her decisions. Instead, ask what your child can do to earn more playing time.

If you do talk to the coach, it should go sort of like this:

Parent: How do you think Dan's been doing on the team?

Coach: He's made some progress.

Parent: Can you tell me what he needs to do to get more playing time?

Coach: His passing skills need work. I've told him that.

Parent: OK, thanks for talking with me.

This approach will at the very least get the coach's attention and may very well result in a little more playing time for your kid without making the coach defensive.

Suzanne Capek Tingley

On the other hand, it may go like this:

> **Parent:** How's Dan been doing this season?
>
> **Coach:** He's doing OK.
>
> **Parent:** What does he need to do to get more playing time?
>
> **Coach:** Keep doing what he's doing.

Or maybe like this:

> **Parent:** What does Dan have to do to get more playing time?
>
> **Coach:** Don't tell me you're another parent who thinks his kid is another Beckham.
>
> **Parent:** What? No! I just would like to see him play more.
>
> **Coach:** Tell him to practice harder.

As I said, no coach is really interested in hearing what you think he should do.

Athletics is one area in which you as a parent will not have much sway – over the coach, that is. But you can have a great amount of influence over how your child feels about his athletic experience. For example, if you don't give your kid a hard time about how much playing time he gets, how he plays when he's on the field or court, and what he needs to do to improve, your child will likely enjoy being part of the team.

The truth is, the coach is right: The vast majority of the kids he sees will not play professional sports. Maybe none of them will. So if your child has the opportunity to work hard, learn some teamwork, and make some friends, he may be OK with the experience.

The bottom line is, playing sports provides a real opportunity for your child to learn some valuable life lessons. The best thing you can do as a parent is to let your child be in charge of this activity.

Now, all the above advice assumes that your child's coach is neither a jerk nor a bully. If your child has a coach that berates the kids, explodes at errors, screams at referees, or manhandles the players, it's a parent's responsibility to take him on.

Start with talking to the coach himself and if you don't get any satisfaction, feel free to move up the chain of command. Sometimes administrators (and parents) turn a blind eye to a coach who wins even if he or she is a bully. Don't put up with it. Talk to the principal, talk to the superintendent, talk to the board of education. Talk to other parents too, but don't be surprised if parents of starters or kids who get a lot of playing time will share your point of view. But high school *isn't* the NBA, and every student deserves to be treated with respect. Intimidators – even intimidators who win – need to be called out.

Most coaches in my experience love the sport and just want to work with kids. They try to be fair, but they're only human and they like to win. They put in hours and hours of their own time (even if they're paid). So support your coach, support your team, and support your child whether she's a starter or a bench warmer. If she's happy, you should be too.

Suzanne Capek Tingley

Chapter 10

If Your Child Is Bullied

There are few things more painful to a parent than watching his or her child become the target of bullying. And there are few things as intolerable as having the teacher or principal say there's nothing he can do about it.

Bullying takes lots of forms in school (and out of school). Physical bullying, intimidation, and extortion are not uncommon and are among the easiest forms of bulling to identify. Social bullying – whispering, exclusion, name calling, shunning – is more difficult to pinpoint but every bit as painful as physical bullying.

Some kids will quickly share with the parents what is happening to them at school. Other children will hide it even from parents out of a sense of shame or fear. If you begin to see changes in your child – silence, withdrawal, general tiredness, for example – talk to your child gently about what's going on. If you child tells you she's being bullied, or if you suspect that may be the case, make an appointment with your child's teacher ASAP.

Many teachers, especially with the heightened sensitivity to bullying we see today, will listen and try to help. However, here are some excuses you may be offered:

- It's just boys being boys.

- Middle school girls are like that sometimes.

- I've never seen it, but I'll keep an eye out. A lot of bullying happens in the halls, at lunch, or in the locker room where we can't see it.

- Sometimes your child makes himself a target with his behavior.

- Bullies just have low self-esteem. Your child should just ignore them.

Accept none of these excuses. Because here's the thing: You have a right to expect that your child will be safe at school. Keeping kids safe is part of the job of school personnel.

Your child's school should have a bullying policy. Indeed, many state departments of education require that all schools adopt a policy and train teachers and kids about bullying. In addition, some states require annual reporting from every school regarding the number and kinds of bullying incidents that have occurred over the year. Check your school's or state's website for guidelines and policies regarding bullying.

Meanwhile, how can you intervene to protect your child? Start with your child's teacher (not the principal), and come with a plan in mind. The conversation should go something like this:

> **Parent:** My son Marco is having a problem with another boy in class.
>
> **Teacher:** What kind of problem?
>
> **Parent:** Bullying. This boy is constantly pushing him, leaning on him, calling him names – just making his life miserable.
>
> **Teacher:** Who is it?
>
> **Parent:** A boy named Irvin.
>
> **Teacher:** Let me talk with your son. I will also talk with Irvin.
>
> **Parent:** OK. Let's start there.
>
> **Teacher:** I will get back to you after I've done that. Let's see how we can fix this.

But what if the teacher says something like this:

> **Teacher:** I've never seen any bullying.

Or:

Teacher: It must be happening outside of my class.

Or:

Teacher: I thought the two of them were friends.

Or:

Teacher: It's pretty hard to keep kids from shoving, bumping into one another, even hitting one another. I'll do my best, but I can't promise anything.

Or:

Teacher: You know, sometimes your son brings it on himself.

If you get any of these responses, here's what you say:

Parent: My child needs to be safe in school. I need to know that we have a plan to keep him safe. What do you think is the best way to proceed?

At this point the teacher may say:

Teacher: Let me talk with your son. And I will talk with Irvin.

Or she may say:

Teacher: I don't know what I can do about something I haven't seen.

If that happens, then you say this:

Parent: I want you to know that I'm going to talk to the principal.

Then do it. Ask the principal to show you the school's policy on bullying and ask what he suggests can be done to keep your child safe. If things don't improve, talk to him again and then prepare to move up the chain of command.

The example I've given here is relatively straightforward. Bullying among boys is often physical or sometimes verbal intimidation. It is reasonably easy to spot, as long as kids are not left unsupervised in locker rooms or halls or lunchrooms.

What is more difficult to deal with is social bullying, often the domain of girls, particularly middle school girls. But note I say "difficult," not "impossible." This is not to say that boys never experience social bullying (nor girls physical bullying), but social bullying tends to be more prevalent among girls. Let me give you an example.

When my younger daughter was in sixth grade, she was a fringe friend to a group of about 5 "popular" girls. Often they included my daughter in the group, but when one of them had a weekend birthday party, Rebecca wasn't invited. That was bad enough, but on the following Monday, all the girls at the party arrived at school in matching purple t-shirts with unicorns on the front and their names on the back.

Rebecca was heartbroken, but that day all of the girls were so nice to her that when she came home, she decided that we should go to the mall and get her a t-shirt just like the others.

"Well, " I said, buying time, "let's see how they treat you by the end of the week."

Later that week another girl in class who apparently had the same idea came to school wearing her own matching shirt. The girls in the group were merciless. They teased her, badgered her, made fun of her, and generally made her life miserable. Rebecca watched in horror, sorry for the girl but so grateful that it wasn't her.

The following day the parents of the targeted girl marched into school to complain about their child being bullied. The principal quickly decided that the girls would not be allowed to wear the shirts to school in the future. It stopped the overt bullying, but it didn't keep the group from shunning the girl.

Some of the best books about female bullying include Rosalind Wiseman's *Queen Bees and Wannabees* (Harmony 2009), Rachel Simmons' *Odd Girl Out* (Harcourt Books 2002), and my personal favorite, Barbara Coloroso's *The Bully, the Bullied, and the Bystander* (Harper Resource 2003). These books are great resources for parents (and school people) for dealing with social aggression in girls.

In her introduction to *Odd Girl Out, the Hidden Culture of Aggression in Girls,* Rachel Simmons talks about being bullied by a group of girls when she was a child and how that experience had stayed with her well into adulthood. In preparation for her book, she gathered similar stories from hundreds of adult women, whose memories of those incidents were as fresh, she says, as if they happened yesterday.

Social bullying can make a young girl's life awful, so awful that she may begin to think that it's not worth living. So if your child is the target, you need to be aggressive in getting the school to deal with it.

What can you do to intervene if your daughter is a target of "the mean girls"? Again, start with your child's teacher, not the principal:

Parent: It appears that a small group of girls has singled my daughter out for harassment.

Teacher: What exactly are they doing?

Parent: They whisper about her, refuse to let her sit at the lunch table, make cracks about her loud enough for her to hear...things like that.

Teacher: These things are often hard to see, but I will talk to your daughter and then with each of the girls.

Parent: That's a start. You'll talk to the girls separately?

Teacher: Yes. That's the best way. Then I will get in touch with you and see what we have to do.

A smart teacher who wants to stop bullying will in fact take action by addressing the problem head on. It is unlikely she sill be completely surprised by your complaint in many cases. Here are some of the things she can do:

- Ask your child to give her specific information about incidents that may have happened.

- Speak to each of the suspected girls individually, not in a group.

- Explain to each of the bullies exactly what will happen if the behavior continues. Consequences may include calling their parents, meeting with the principal, even suspension from school.

- Explain to each girl that the teacher will be aware of any girl(s) encouraging others to participate in bullying.

•Make sure every girl knows that the teacher and the school take bullying seriously and won't tolerate it.

Be prepared for what often happens in these cases: Active bullying stops, but your child may not be included in the group. There is nothing you can do about that painful exclusion. You can make them stop targeting your child, but you cannot make them include her. However, once the bullying stops and the mean girls move on to other activities (or other targets), your child can move on also.

During this period keep a close eye on your child's computer activity because kids will often move the bullying to the Internet if it is shut down at school. If this happens, go back to the principal and work with her to get the parents of the bullies involved. Depending on the severity of the bullying and the cooperation of the other parents, you may have to contact the police.

The bottom line is that bullying is not a joking matter, and parents need to insist that the school take it seriously. The days of "just ignore it" are long gone, and schools must be responsive to complaints.

Remember that schools in many states must file with the state education department an annual report on bullying incidents and their consequences. Do not accept any excuses from school personnel when it comes to protecting your child from bullying.If you get no response as you move up the chain of command, contact your state education department.

Just a little endnote about the mean girls in my daughter's sixth grade class. That spring another mother and I coached our daughters' recreational soccer team. We won a few games, lost a

Suzanne Capek Tingley

few games, and everybody played. Our last game of the season was against the mean girls' team, coached by the father of one of them. They had won all their games. Our team played the best game of their season, leading by 1 goal for the majority of the game. But with 5 minutes to go, the other team scored. That's when their coach yelled to his girls, "If you get your foot on the ball, kick it as hard as you can out of bounds!" (in kids soccer, the clock doesn't stop when you have to chase the ball out of bounds). In other words, run down the clock instead of giving our girls a chance to play the ball and win the game.

Synecdoche: A part of the whole that represents the whole.

Suzanne Capek Tingley

Chapter 11

When You Have to Move Up the Administrative Ladder

It's important for parents to know that you always have the right to move up the administrative ladder or chain of command if you're unhappy with a teacher's decision regarding your child.

Just to review, that public school chain is similar to this in most states:

Teacher

Department Head/Grade Supervisor

Assistant Principal/Principal

Assistant Superintendent/Superintendent

Local Board of Education

State Education Commissioner

State Board of Education

You can also throw in for good measure various civil courts. For the most part, your chances for success in getting what you want for your child can be improved if you follow the chain of command – not necessarily every single step, but in ascending order.

On garden-variety issues, beginning at the lowest level with the person who can actually solve the problem is usually the best way to go. If you are unsatisfied with that person's decision, tell him or her that you plan to talk to the person at the next level and then do it.

Pressing forward with your argument means that you need to be prepared with facts – test scores, eyewitness accounts, local school law, state law – whatever you need to prove your point. You want to present a rational argument for your position, not an emotional rant.

Let's look at an example. Your child is in third grade and has poor reading skills. His math skills are good, but his teacher wants to retain him. You do not believe retention is good educational practice and would prefer that your child be promoted and receive additional reading help.

His teacher is adamant that your child repeat third grade. You've had numerous conversations with her to no effect. You make an appointment with the principal and you thoughtfully and civilly present your point of view:

- You note that your child does well in math and is a year behind in reading.

- You question why he needs to repeat an entire year when he knows, his teacher knows, and you know that his specific problem is reading

- You ask that your child be tested for a learning disability. You say that you understand that the district must comply within 30 days of your request according to federal guidelines (Individuals with Educational Disabilities Act, often referred to as IDEA).

- You say that you understand that if your child is found to have a disability, he qualifies for extra help (resource room) and should move on to fourth grade.

- You note that if he doesn't have a learning disability, you will want to know what other kinds of extra help are available.

- You cite the research that confirms that children who are held back are more likely to drop out of school before finishing high school. You ask for the school's research to support retention.

- You request a copy of the appeals process.

•You point out that your child is already bigger than most kids in his grade.

•You advise school personnel that you will move up the ladder if you need to.

You see the process. You need to come armed with solid information that supports your argument.

Here's a point you rarely want to use as your main argument:

Parent: I'm not just advocating for my child, but for EVERY child in this situation.

In my 25 years as an administrator, I've heard dozens of parents lay claim to this altruistic position with great sincerity. However, it's really OK if you are just here about your own kid. If you don't advocate for him, who will? You don't need to contend that you're actually worried about everyone else.

Just for the record and as a little diversion, here's my other favorite questionable altruistic comment: "I'm doing this so I can give back to the community."

I once sat on an interview committee for a position that paid a great deal of money and carried a good share of local power. I asked the same question of all three finalists for the position:

Me: Please tell the committee why you want this job.

First Candidate: I think I have the skills for this job and I'd look forward to the challenge.

Me: Sounds reasonable.

Second Candidate: I've always wanted to work in this location because it's where I grew up and I have family here. And the job would be fun and challenging.

Me: Sounds reasonable.

Third Candidate: I just want to give back to the community that has given me so much.

Me: I'm going to press a button now that will make your chair shoot you like a cannonball through the window.

So the moral of the story is not to try to con anyone ever with fake altruism. It's unbecoming and tends to make your listeners feel that you think they may be gullible.

How far should you go up the administrative ladder? Short answer: As far as you think you have to in order to get what your child needs.

Let's say you've talked to the teacher and the principal and have had no success in changing their minds about an issue regarding your child. Should you accept the decision or continue up the ladder? Let's look at a few examples.

Suppose the coach of the varsity soccer team regularly allows girls who don't come to practice to start anyway because they're good players. Your daughter goes to every practice and is never allowed to start. Even if the principal doesn't agree with the coach's decision, it's unlikely that he will intervene on your daughter's behalf. And frankly, neither will the school board as both will say that while it may be unfair, the coach has a right to play whom he wants.

Now suppose the coach regularly has some of these starters over to his house for a beer after the game. Time to move up the ladder.

Let's look at another example. Suppose children have to take a test to be allowed into the gifted program. Your child scores one point below the cut-off. The principal says there has to be a line somewhere and refuses to allow your child into the program even though one point has no statistical significance. Time to move up the ladder.

Here's another situation. Suppose your child and a few of her friends are high at the first school dance of the year. Consequently they are banned from all school activities for the rest of the year. The school quarterback did the same thing last year and was suspended for just one game. Time to move up the ladder to challenge this arbitrary decision.

Now suppose your child has been late 15 times over the past semester. Every time she's late she has to make up the time after school. Stay right where you are and take stock of what she's doing (and what you're doing).

Suppose your child hits another child on the bus over the head with his history book and is suspended from riding the bus for a week. Warm up the car if it's too far to walk.

The bottom line is, don't threaten anybody and remain civil. If you think your child's rights have been violated, request a meeting with the school board. Get a lawyer if you need to. Move on to the state education commissioner. It's your right as a parent, as a citizen, as a taxpayer. Remember that not every teacher, principal, or board of education makes the right decision every time. Use common sense, careful argument, and evidence when you present your case. Refuse to be intimidated, but remain civil.

Suzanne Capek Tingley

Chapter 12

Where Does the Buck Stop?

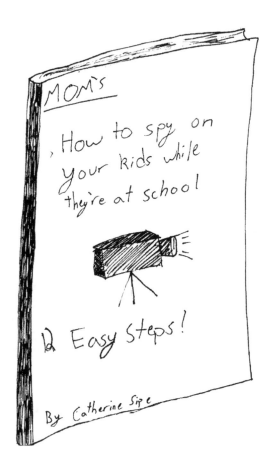

How much support does your child need to be successful on her own? When should you let her make her own decisions? How can you help her be responsible, yet independent? When, if ever, should you let her fail?

Tough questions. Let's start with parental support. Listening to your child, asking questions, remembering what he's told you, and being slow to criticize (both your child and his teachers) are essential parenting skills.

It's also a good idea to remember that actions really do speak louder than words, so every time your child performs on stage or on a field or court you need to make every effort to be there. I know – you have other responsibilities, including a job. Emergencies arise, sickness – yours or someone else's – strikes. You have a conflict with another child's activity. Maybe you're deployed or your spouse is deployed and you are doing the best you can. The point is, though, if you are able to make it, you need to be there. Kids will get over the occasional absence if you're there every time you can be.

You might be surprised at how many parents of students in the upper elementary grades begin to back off from school events like parent conferences, open houses, or math fun nights. When I was an elementary principal, some parents routinely dropped their kids off for music performances and picked them up afterwards. From middle school through high school, some parents never watch their kid play or perform. My guess is, if you're reading this book, you are not that parent.

Also, if you're reading this book, you probably aren't the parent who attends sporting events but regularly harasses the officials. Likewise, you're probably not the parent who makes a scene at a concert like the guy at the middle school orchestra program I attended the other night.

The concert was held in the gym, and as you may have noticed, some people think that no matter what the event, if it's held in the gym, it's OK for the audience to act as if it's a basketball game. In other words, it's fine to cheer or yell out to your child or talk throughout the whole performance. One way to curtail this behavior is to shut off the lights where the audience sits (a move that suggests an auditorium), but apparently the local administrators weren't aware of this trick. So a dad who apparently had to leave the concert early felt it was completely appropriate for him to boogie his way across the floor as if the orchestra were playing a dance number just for him.

Well, at least his kid knew he was there.

As I said, some parents believe that their children need them less after elementary school. Nothing could be farther from the truth. They may act like they don't need you or want you around, but believe me, they need you now as much as they ever did. Even if you boogie your way out of the gym.

As your child moves through middle and high school, know when report cards come out. Put the dates on your calendar so that you'll know if the report card doesn't arrive. Stay on top of your child's grades and encourage him to participate in at least some school activities. He doesn't need to be an athlete or a music star. There are many extracurricular school activities that don't require any special skills besides attendance and interest.

Know who your child's friends are. Volunteer to drive your child and her friends to school activities or pick them up. Encourage your child to invite friends over. Take the time to meet with your child's teachers and introduce yourself to the principal. You don't have to be a room mother or PTA president, but you might find some time to volunteer for career days or field days. You might join the band boosters or the sports boosters or the Odyssey of the Mind group or the Special

Olympics group. You can even help organize one of the hundreds of sales campaigns kids now have to participate in to augment the school budget.

Volunteering at school keeps you involved in your child's education. In addition, teachers and administrators who know you and your child are more likely to be cooperative and helpful when you need to meet with them about a school issue.

Most parents back off from monitoring their child's homework, papers, and projects as the child moves through the upper grades and shows herself capable of handling her own school responsibilities. Backing off doesn't mean ignoring; it's fine to talk to your child about when work is due and about how she feels she's handling her courses even in the upper grades.

As your child moves through secondary school, do not abdicate your responsibility to make sure that she is enrolled in the best program for her. Don't allow her to shy away from challenging courses, especially if her reason for not taking a tough course is to protect her class rank (not as important as a transcript showing rigorous course work). Attend any program meetings your school may offer, and sign up to meet with your child's counselor (along with your child) when it comes time to schedule the next year's classes.

Most parents are very active participants when it comes to helping their child choose a college or other post-secondary program. Some even take it upon themselves to help write their child's college essay. You do not need to do that, nor should you. What you may want to do, however, is sit down with your child and schedule on her calendar and yours when she's going to take the PSAT, the SAT, or the ACT. Do not rely on your child's school counselor to remind your child and everyone else's child when applications or financial aid forms are due. Some counselors have hundreds of students to advise and it's easy for your child to miss a deadline. You need to stay on top of the paperwork because even the most organized kids tend to get stressed out as graduation approaches and need a guiding hand.

If you child chooses a tech school or the military or even (gasp!) a real job, be there to support his choice. The first post-secondary choice (even if it is college) is not necessarily the right one nor the one your child will stick with.

One of the hardest things for parents to decide as their child becomes older is when to intervene and when to let the child take responsibility for herself. Here are three thoughts to keep in mind when making this decision:

> •If it's an academic issue, your job is to determine if your child is getting appropriate instruction, is placed in the right class, and is receiving any extra help she needs. Your job is also to make sure that she is doing her part in preparing for class.

> •If it's a disciplinary issue, let your child take responsibility for her behavior. Your role as the parent is to make sure that discipline is fair rather than arbitrary, and that it is applied evenly. Of course, it goes without saying that you are your child's first disciplinarian.

> •If it's a social issue, your job is to protect your child by ensuring that your child's school is a safe environment. Sometimes that means encouraging school officials to take a stand; other times it means forcing them to do so.

And then, as every parent knows, despite our most careful planning, there are small surprises like this to deal with:

Kid: We're finishing our unit on dinosaurs tomorrow.

Mom: Was it fun?

Kid: Yes! And to celebrate we're having a dinosaur party tomorrow. I told my teacher my mom could make a pterodactyl cake.

Mom: What??!!

Kid: A cake shaped like a pterodactyl. The flying dinosaur. It will be so cool.

Mom: It's 10:00 at night!

Kid: But I said you'd do it.

I don't know what you would do, but at 2 AM I'm frosting a cake that looks *nothing* like a flying dinosaur except that it is green, which I hope is an acceptable color for pterodactyls.

In the morning, the kid looks at it and says, "Awesome!" I think, *my work here is done.*

It isn't, of course.

I'm not recommending that every time your child makes a rash promise you have to make good on it. There are lots of other ways to be a part of your child's ongoing education. Even so, occasionally you'll have the opportunity to look like a hero.

Finally, if you really want to make a difference in your child's schooling, run for the Board of Education.

I should warn you, being on a board of education takes a great deal of time and commitment. You will need to read and study and attend conferences. You are expected to show up at important school events like graduation. It's not for the faint of heart because not all of your community members will embrace and support the decisions you will have to make. In addition, unhappy parents, particularly those whose children have been involved in a disciplinary matter, are free to go to the local papers or television stations and present their version of events that will often make you look like a fool, a dolt, or even a foolish dolt. You, however, will not be able to defend yourself because you will be bound by rules of confidentiality.

You will also be the recipient of many, many calls from irate parents complaining about everything from budget to snow days to teachers to coaches to playgrounds...you name it, someone will complain about it. You will need to develop great listening skills and a thick skin.

Still, as part of a board, you will have the opportunity to guide the school in a direction that will benefit students. One of the most important functions of a school board is to choose the superintendent and to monitor her or his progress. (In my humble opinion, some boards today abdicate that authority and act as if they work for the superintendent, not the other way around). You will also vote to approve the budget and the main administrative and department hires in a district, so the board wields substantial power in setting the course for the district.

On the other hand, be aware that the board is powerful only when it acts as a whole. As an individual board member, you have no more influence over what happens in the district than anyone else. In fact, if you are a parent, you may have a little less power because you don't want to be seen as trying to influence outcomes for your personal child because you are a board member. When my husband was on the school board for our local district, for example, I was the parent who regularly dealt with teachers and school issues so that he could not be accused of using his board member status to unfair advantage.

Of course, not everyone has the time, energy, nor desire to run for the board. For most parents, just making sure your child is getting what she needs from her local school is enough. To do that, we don't need to be (nor should we want to be) "helicopter parents," always hovering just outside the classroom, ready to swoop in at a moment's notice to rescue our child from whatever occurs. Instead, we could be more like "pterodactyl parents," slower to get off the ground, more ponderous, but formidable when we appear. In my mind I see pterodactyls needing a very long runway.

One of our major goals as parents is, after all, to foster strong and caring relationships between teachers and students. As David L. Kirp, a professor at Berkley, says, "All youngsters need to believe that they have a stake in the future, a goal worth striving for, if they're going to make it in school. They need a champion, someone who believes in them, and that's where teachers enter the picture" (*Teaching Is Not a Business*, New York Times, August 17, 2014).

If we are lucky, as adults we can remember teachers who made a difference in our lives. They did more than teach us the causes of the Civil War or the properties of an isosceles triangle or the theme of *A Separate Peace*. They connected with us as individuals. They liked us, joked with us, supported us, and believed in us. They encouraged us to try. In turn, we confided in them and we trusted them. They were adults we could talk to when we didn't want to talk to our parents, yet we never doubted that they supported our parents.

Interestingly enough, special teachers like these don't even have to teach your favorite subject. One of my favorite middle school teachers taught science, not English, and I didn't excel in science. My younger daughter selected as her high school advisor her physical education teacher, who never coached her sports teams; my older daughter loved her fourth grade teacher who went on to become a well-known children's author. Kids and teachers connect for various reasons, and we're glad they do.

From very early in their schooling, children respond to the warmth and acceptance of their teachers. These bonds are the real "value added" in schools, for without these connections kids don't see any value at all in school nor a reason to be there.

I am reminded of my three-year-old granddaughter who cried every day when her mother dropped her off at pre-school. The child was expected to enter the classroom, put her things in her cubby, and take her seat at the puzzle table. She cried throughout the whole routine. And she wasn't the only one.

Then one morning when she arrived at school her teacher called out, "Good morning, Piper! We are so happy you're here. Take off your coat and come join us at the table!"

The tears stopped. Piper let go of her mother's hand, dropped her coat in her cubby, and ran to the table. The new routine of greeting the children worked not only for Piper, but for the rest of the kids as well.

Kids want to be recognized and acknowledged just like everyone else. I know teachers from elementary school to high school who stand outside their classroom doors every day before class begins and greet each student by name as he or she enters. Students don't feel anonymous in those classes.

Not every student is so lucky. I was once called for grand jury duty, and I was struck by the number of young men – boys, really - who appeared before the court. In a case involving an armed robbery a seventeen-year-old testified that he didn't have a gun himself, but he did see a gun in "one of those bags like those high school kids use for gym." He was the same age as "those high school kids," but he had dropped out and clearly felt that he and those kids had nothing in common, least of all school.

Those strong, positive bonds that students and teachers forge are essential not only for learning, but for commitment to the process. They give kids a personal stake in their own education and a belief that they can succeed. Those bonds may be what keep some kids in school. So as parents we want to encourage connections between our kids and those in charge of their education. We can foster those relationships by getting to know their teachers, administrators, and all the other school personnel with whom our children interact in the course of a day. We should treat them with and talk about them with respect, especially in front of our children.

This does not mean that we accept poor instruction, shoddy discipline, or questionable administrative decisions. There will be individuals or situations that will try our patience and our good will. Yet how we respond to those individuals or situations can have an effect on our child's total educational experience and attitude towards all school personnel.

Suzanne Capek Tingley

You can get what your child needs and deserves from your local school by being informed about what your child is doing and what the school in providing. You can help shape the mission of the school and you can influence its daily operating procedures. You can make sure your child is being appropriately challenged or is receiving the extra help she needs. All of this takes time and effort, but few things are more important than your child's education.

Suzanne Capek Tingley

Chapter 13

Checking for Understanding

Perhaps you remember way back in Chapter 1, I mentioned a teaching technique called, "wait time." Giving students time to think about an answer instead of making every discussion a lightning round improves the discourse and doesn't make kids panicky if an answer doesn't immediately come to mind.

Another helpful technique is "checking for understanding." Teachers can ask students about what they have just talked about so that the teacher can gauge how effective her teaching has been. So let's try a little checking to see how I've done. You'll notice that since this book is for smart parents, some of the scenarios require application of information, not rote answers (not that there's anything wrong with rote learning, of course.)

1. You think your child's teacher is giving her too much homework. She's only in third grade and she's working at least an hour every night. The best thing to do is

> **A.** Go directly to the principal to complain. After all, he's supposed to be in charge.

> **B.** Make an appointment to talk to the teacher. Maybe it's the homework, or maybe your child is taking longer than most kids.

> **C.** See what parents of other kids think. Maybe you can get a whole group together.

Answer: B. Always start with the lowest rung on the ladder if it's a person who can solve the problem. You can always move up to the principal if you are not satisfied with the teacher's response. You can check with other parents, but you don't need a posse to talk to your child's teacher.

2. Your child is starting in a new middle school and she didn't receive dress code information with her enrollment packet. You are wondering what to buy for your child to wear to school. The best way to find out about the dress code is

> **A.** Wait until your child violates it.

B. Call the main office.

C. Talk to neighbors or other parents.

Answer: B. If you didn't get a copy of the dress code at the beginning of the year, call the office and ask for one. If there is no dress code and kids wear whatever they want, you may eventually want to talk to the principal about whether it would be a good idea to have some guidelines, especially if what students are allowed to wear (or not allowed to wear) concerns you. You might also check with other parents to see what most kids wear.

I should point out, though, that when I was a superintendent in upstate New York where the average snowfall was 140 inches, kids still occasionally chose to come to school in shorts and flip-flops during the winter. Good to know, but maybe not for your kid.

3. When your child's teacher tells you that homework is 30% of your child's final grade, you should say

A. Are you kidding me? The grade is supposed to reflect mastery, not diligence!

B. Can we make it 60%?

C. I though homework was part of the effort grade.

Answer: The grade *is* supposed to reflect mastery, but let's not be confrontational, so forget A. Answer B speaks to the arbitrariness of including homework at all and can be said with a touch of humor. Best to go with **C**, but if the conversation goes well, you may want to bring up the ideas raised in A and B. Nicely.

4. Parent-teacher conferences are coming up but you will be out of town on business and your spouse has to work during the conference days. Your child is doing very well and you really think that you won't hear anything new anyway. You should

> **A.** Call or email the teacher, explain your family's situation, and ask if you should meet with her at a later time convenient to both of you.

> **B.** Cancel your plans to be out of town.

> **C.** Forget it this time. If there's a problem, they'll let you know.

Answer: A. Contact the teacher so she knows you're not ignoring conference time. If she needs to talk to you, she will let you know.

5. You run into your child's teacher at a large dinner party hosted by a mutual friend. During dinner the conversation turns to the local school system and teachers in general. One guest is particularly critical of teachers, unions, and their "easy" jobs that give them summers off. "After all," he says, "anyone can teach." What's the best thing for you to do?

> **A.** Say nothing at dinner, but catch you child's teacher later before she leaves and tell her your child is having a great year.

B. Tell the guy to put a sock in it. If it's so easy, how come he's not doing it?

C. Tactfully, and maybe humorously, disagree, noting that it's pretty important that our kids have great teachers and like lots of things, it's not as easy as it looks.

Answer: It's not unusual for conversations like this to come up in social situations, especially over the past few years when teachers have been targets of many reformers. It will not endear you to your child's teacher to sit silently while her profession is criticized. Still, you don't want to insult anyone or start a battle.

The best answer is **C** if you can pull it off. You could say something like, "John, we all have to admit if it weren't for our teachers, we wouldn't be sitting here enjoying this lovely dinner." If you can't muster that up, just say, "I can't agree. We've been very pleased with our schools. How 'bout those Patriots?"

By the way, Taylor Mali, teacher turned slam poet, has a great take on this scenario from a dinner party he attended. One of the guests asked him what he makes. See a video of his Ted Talk and prepare to be amused here:

http://www.ted.com/talks/taylor_mali_what_teachers_make

6. Your twelve-year-old son has been the target of a group of bullies. They slam his locker closed, shove him in the halls, call him sexually charged names, and generally make life tough for him. You've talked to the teacher and basically the boys have backed off during school. The problem now is the bus, where they continue to harass your child. You've been to the principal.

The bus driver claims to have seen nothing, so the principal says he has no real evidence that the boys are bullying your child. What do you do next?

A. Call the police. What these kids are doing is at least a misdemeanor and they should be arrested.

B. Drive your child to school and back.

C. Tell the principal that your child has a right to be safe at school and that if he isn't willing to do anything about the bus problems, you will go to the superintendent.

Answer: While you may end up dealing with the police, at this point you should still try to work with the school people. Ask if seats can be assigned on the bus so that the bullies don't sit together and your child doesn't sit near any of them. This is an easy fix and doesn't cost anything. Ask if the principal can meet with the bullies individually not to accuse them, but to put them on notice.

Stop at the bus garage and talk to the director of transportation about the problem. Talk to her about the driver's insistence that she hasn't seen anything. If the principal and the director are unwilling to take action, move up the chain of command until you get what your child needs.

Yes, you could drive your child to school, but that action singles him out and relieves the school of its legal obligation to keep kids safe. The answer is **C**.

7. Your child has been slowly falling behind in primary school and is now in third grade. Every year you talked with her teacher about her progress and whether she needs extra help. Each year her teacher has assured you that it was just a question of maturation and that your child would soon catch up with her peers. She is now a year behind in reading and beginning to show reluctance to get up for school in the morning. At parent conferences, her teacher said she is thinking of recommending your daughter for retention. What should you do?

A. Ask that your child be tested for learning disabilities before you make any decision and make sure that the teacher knows that you know the school has thirty days to honor your request.

B. Consider whether having her repeat third grade would be a good idea. She's small for her age anyway, and it would give her a year to catch up.

C. Get her a private tutor.

Answer: A. The first thing to do is determine why your child has fallen behind and what can be done to help her catch up. If testing shows that she has a learning disability, she qualifies for additional help. If it shows she is a slow learner, she may not qualify for resource room, but the school may offer other kinds of academic assistance.

Some children indeed benefit from a private tutor or private learning agencies, but first make sure that the school has done due diligence in providing for your child's learning needs. Simply repeating the same grade with the same kind of instruction will not magically benefit your child.

8. Your middle school student is expected to sell candy and wrapping paper to raise funds for his class trip to Washington, D. C. next spring to see the cherry blossoms and tour the White House. The amount each child sells will be deducted from each individual's cost. What's the best way to handle this project?

> **A.** Take the sales information to work, call your relatives, and sell as much as you can.

> **B.** Buy it all yourself.

> **C.** Buy a few things for the family, but tell your child you expect him to call his grandparents, aunts and uncles, or neighbors himself as his contribution to the trip.

Answer: Don't you wish you didn't have to do any of these things – that schools could just afford field trips without having to raise the money? Yeah, me too. But it's nearly impossible that your child will escape some kind of fundraising during his years in school.

It's important to remember that it's not your trip; it's his. So let him take the responsibility of making some contacts himself with family or neighbors. It's tempting to avoid the whole business and buy the stuff yourself, but then you'd like the parents who do their kids' science projects or demonstrations. So help your kid make some contacts, and hope that future fundraisers will include something you'd actually like or use. Florida grapefruit and oranges, anybody? The answer is **C.**

9. Your daughter's advanced math teacher calls you to complain that your daughter has been disrespectful to him. You ask for specifics, and he tells you some of the responses she has given him in class. They don't sound that bad to you, but he says it's the demeanor and tone of voice that are inappropriate. You talk to your daughter and she says, "I'm not disrespectful to Mr. Ogdon. I'm just not respectful. He's kind of a jerk." What's your response?

A. While you think that she's pretty smart to make the distinction, she needs to improve her demeanor.

B. She's right; Mr. O has the reputation of being kind of a jerk to kids. But she needs to be respectful in class because nobody wants to be disrespected in front of others, least of all a teacher.

C. Whatever his reputation, he's the teacher and if she can't respect him she better drop the course.

Answer: A and **B.** It's a life lesson; there will always be people that you will find challenging, but you still have to be able to work with them.

10. You are in a professional meeting when you are interrupted by a call from your high school daughter at the Hague, where she is attending a Model United Nations conference with members of her school club (lots of grapefruit and oranges, believe me!). Your heart rolls over. You excuse yourself and pick up the phone. "Mom," she says, "Donna and I met these really nice waiters yesterday at dinner. They would like to take us on a tour of the city tomorrow. Our chaperone says absolutely not. Could you talk to her and tell her it's OK with you?" What's your answer?

A. Are you out of your mind?

B. Absolutely not!

C. No. No. No. And let me talk to your advisor right now.

Answer: All of the above. This is a fun story to tell today now that she has her own daughters.

I'm sure you did very well in determining the best course of action in these little scenarios. Of course, it's much easier in retrospect to know the answers, and I'm sure as a parent you could add quite a few scenarios of your own. Hang on to them; write them down. They make great stories when your children have children of their own -- and their children have their own school experiences.

Suzanne Capek Tingley

REFERENCES

Ballow, Elizabeth (2014). *Richmond's Maggie L. Walker Governor's School Protested Dress Code Sexism in the Best Way.* Retrieved from www.Bustle.org.

Brown, Emma (2014). *Test Data Show Link Between Students' Scores, and Absence Rates.* Retrieved from www.WashingtonPost.com.

Gladwell, Malcolm. *Outliers: The Story of Success.* New York: Little, Brown, and Company, 2007.

Kirp, David L. (2014). *Teaching is Not a Business.* New York Times, August 17.

Mali, Taylor (2003). *What Teachers Make.* Retrieved from www.red.com/talks/taylor_mali_what_teachers_make.

Toppo, Greg (2014). *Homework Load Little Changed in 30 Years, Study Says.* Retrieved from www.USATODAY.com.

Suzanne Capek Tingley

SPECIAL THANKS

TINA RODRIGUEZ
KELSEY JOHNSON

SCHOOL OF ART, WILLIAMSBURG, VA

Suzanne Capek Tingley

ABOUT THE AUTHOR

Suzanne Capek Tingley has been a teacher, principal, superintendent, and adjunct professor in education administration. She is also an educational writer and consultant. She is the mother of two adult children. Her work has appeared in many national educational journals. She created a series of educational videos for Magna Publications and was a blogger for Scholastic Administrator for several years. Her awards include an "Outstanding Administrator Award" from the New York State Library Media Specialists Association and a "Woman of Distinction Award" from the New York State Senate. This is her second book about improving relationships between parents and schools.

Suzanne Capek Tingley

18793864R00079

Made in the USA
Middletown, DE
21 March 2015